# Revise THE NATIONAL TESTS

SCIENCE KEY STAGE 3

**Bob McDuell**
**Graham Booth**
**David Baylis**

# Contents

Letts

# What you need to know

**1** Many animals and plants have **organs** that help them to carry out life processes. For example, an ovary produces eggs for reproduction.

**2** Not all animals and plants have organs but they are all made up of **cells**.

**3** A cell is made from **cytoplasm** and a **nucleus**.

**4** A **cell membrane** is found at the outer surface of the cytoplasm in all cells. The cell membrane controls what can get into and out of the cell.

| organ | function |
|---|---|
| brain | coordination |
| windpipe | carries air to and from lungs |
| lung | gas exchange |
| heart | pumps blood |
| stomach | stores and digests food |
| kidney | removes wastes from the blood |

**5** The **cytoplasm** of a cell is the place where the chemical changes that keep the cell alive take place.

**6** A cell **nucleus** contains genetic material. It controls the chemical activity of the cell.

**7** Plant cells differ from animal cells in that they have **cell walls** and some have **chloroplasts**.

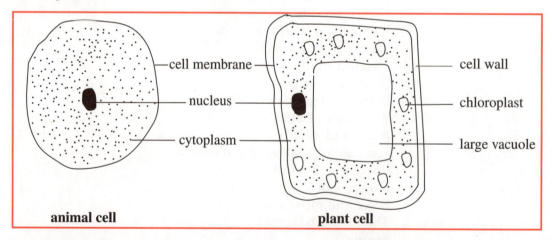

animal cell          plant cell

**8** The wall of a plant cell is found outside the cell membrane. It is made from **cellulose**. The wall helps to support the cell and keep its shape.

**9** **Chloroplasts** contain **chlorophyll**. They trap light for use in **photosynthesis**.

**10** Different types of cells have different jobs to do. The cells are **adapted**, showing special features that help them to carry out particular functions.

| cell | adaptation | function |
|------|-----------|----------|
| egg | stored food | support embryo |
| sperm | tail | swim to egg |
| leaf palisade cell | large number of chloroplasts | photosynthesis |
| root hair cell | large surface area | absorption of water and minerals |
| xylem cell | waterproofed walls | transport of water and minerals |

*Some important body structures of man*

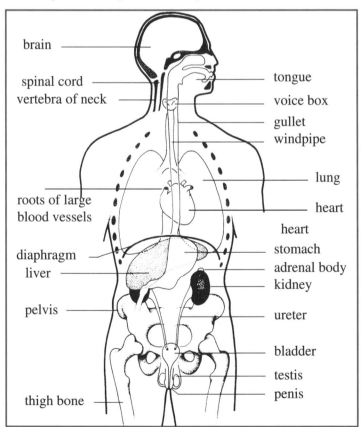

brain
spinal cord
vertebra of neck
roots of large blood vessels
diaphragm
liver
pelvis
thigh bone
tongue
voice box
gullet
windpipe
lung
heart
heart
stomach
adrenal body
kidney
ureter
bladder
testis
penis

## Quick Questions

1   Which organ stores urine?
2   What is the basic unit of living things?
3   What are the two basic parts of any cell?
4   Which structure contains the cytoplasm of a cell?
5   What goes on in the cytoplasm of a cell?
6   What is the function of a cell nucleus?
7   Describe two ways in which plant cells differ from animal cells.
8   Why is cellulose an important chemical in plant cell structure?
9   Where is chlorophyll concentrated in plant cells?
10  How is a sperm adapted to do its job?

# What you need to know

**1** The human diet contains **carbohydrates**, **proteins**, **fats**, **minerals**, **vitamins**, **fibre** and **water**.

**2** A **balanced diet** provides the correct amounts of carbohydrates, proteins, fats, etc. to meet a particular individual's needs.

**3** Some foods do not contain all of the components listed in 1 above. It is important therefore that humans eat a variety of foods.

**4** Carbohydrates and fats may be used as **fuel**. Energy is released from them during **respiration**. The energy is used to keep the body working.

**5** Food provides the chemical building blocks for growth and repair.

**6** Most of the molecules in human food are too big to pass through the membranes lining the gut. **Digestion** makes them smaller, allowing them to be absorbed.

**7** **Enzymes** released into the gut speed up the digestion of food. Each enzyme will work on one type of food molecule only.

**8** The small, soluble molecules formed during digestion are **absorbed** in the small **intestine** into the blood system. They are then transported in the blood to cells elsewhere in the body and put to use.

**9** Some of the molecules in food that humans eat are not digested. These molecules and other, waste materials are lost from the body as faeces. This process is called **egestion**.

**10** **Blood** provides an important transport medium for digested food, respiratory gases, waste products and hormones. Materials 'get on and off' the transport system at thin-walled, 'leaky' blood vessels called capillaries.

*The process of digestion*

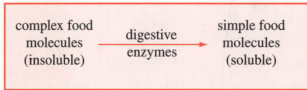

complex food molecules (insoluble) → digestive enzymes → simple food molecules (soluble)

## Key concept

The tables show good sources for particular food materials and examples of enzyme-controlled digestion.

| Food material | Source |
|---|---|
| carbohydrate (starch) | potatoes, rice, wheat flour |
| carbohydrate (glucose) | grapes |
| fat | milk, butter |
| protein | lean meat, cheese |
| vitamin C | citrus fruits |
| vitamin D | dairy products |
| calcium | dairy products |
| dietary fibre | vegetable matter |

| food | enzyme | product |
|---|---|---|
| starch | amylase | maltose |
| proteins | proteases | amino acids |
| fats | lipases | fatty acids and glycerol |

*The diagram shows how different foods are transported away from the small intestine after absorption.*

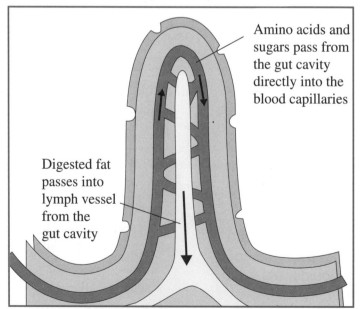

Amino acids and sugars pass from the gut cavity directly into the blood capillaries

Digested fat passes into lymph vessel from the gut cavity

## Quick Questions

1 Carbohydrates, fats, minerals, fibre and water are five essential components of a balanced diet. Name two more.

2 What must be true for an individual's diet to be a balanced one?

3 Why is it important to try to eat a range of different types of food?

4 Which type of food chemicals would you recommend someone to eat if they were doing a lot of physical work?

5 Food provides the energy to do work. Name two other processes for which food supplies the raw materials.

6 Why do we have to digest our food?

7 Enzymes are sometimes called 'biological catalysts'. Explain why this is an appropriate description.

8 Where does most digested food get into the human blood system?

9 Suggest a reason why some of the chemicals, e.g. cellulose, in our food are not digested .

10 In what way are blood capillaries important in the human transport system?

## What you need to know

1   **Skeletons** support the body, protect vital organs, provide anchor points for muscles and are jointed, allowing movement to take place.

2   There are three types of **joints** present in the human skeleton. These are immovable joints, e.g. in the skull, slightly movable joints, e.g. between the vertebrae in the spine, and freely movable joints, e.g. elbow and shoulder.

3   A **muscle** is attached to a bone at each end by **tendons**. Tendons are not elastic. When the muscle contracts the two bones are pulled closer to each other.

4   **Bones** are attached to each other at a joint, by **ligaments** which are tough, fibrous structures that can stretch a little. The job of ligaments is to prevent the joint from dislocating.

5   The elbow is a **hinge** joint. This type of joint allows movement in one plane only. The shoulder is a **ball-and-socket** joint. This is more flexible and allows movement in several planes.

| type of joint | position |
|---|---|
| immovable | skull, bones of pelvis |
| slightly movable | between vertebrae |
| freely movable: hinge; ball and socket | elbow, knee hip, shoulder |

6   Friction in a joint is reduced by **cartilage** and in some cases by **synovial fluid** as well.

7   A muscle can do work, e.g. move a bone, only when it contracts. It does not reverse the change when it relaxes. Another muscle is needed to do that.

8   Muscles are usually found in pairs having opposite effects. They are described as **antagonistic muscles**.

9   The **biceps** is attached to the humerus at one end and to the ulna at the other. The **triceps** is attached to the humerus and the scapula (shoulder blade) at one end and to the ulna at the other.

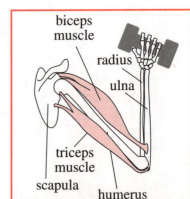

**10** Contraction of the biceps bends the arm at the elbow joint. Contraction of the triceps straightens the arm.

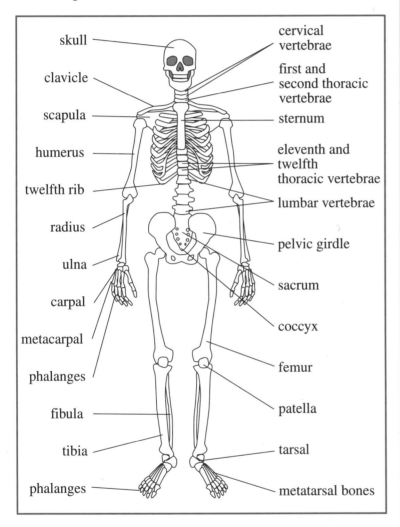

| | |
|---|---|
| skull | cervical vertebrae |
| clavicle | first and second thoracic vertebrae |
| scapula | sternum |
| humerus | eleventh and twelfth thoracic vertebrae |
| twelfth rib | lumbar vertebrae |
| radius | pelvic girdle |
| ulna | sacrum |
| carpal | coccyx |
| metacarpal | femur |
| phalanges | patella |
| fibula | |
| tibia | tarsal |
| phalanges | metatarsal bones |

**Key concept**

Muscles do work when they contract – they cannot do work when they relax.

## Quick Questions

1 Name one example where the human skeleton shows a protective function.

2 The skeleton protects vital organs. Name two other functions.

3 Which structures attach muscles to bones?

4 What normally prevents a joint from dislocating?

5 The elbow is a hinge joint. Name another hinge joint in the human skeleton.

6 What is the difference between a hinge joint and a ball-and-socket joint?

7 Sometimes the cartilage in a joint is damaged. How does this affect the efficiency of the joint?

8 Why is it necessary to have a pair of muscles working antagonistically at a joint?

9 Which muscle bends the arm at the human elbow joint?

10 Name the three bones to which the human triceps is attached.

## What you need to know

1 Boys start to produce sperm somewhere between the ages of twelve and sixteen. Girls start to release eggs a little earlier, between the ages of eleven and fifteen. This stage in human development is called **puberty**.

2 **Secondary sexual characteristics** develop during adolescence, the stage in development between puberty and sexual maturity.

3 Both sexes begin to show a greater interest in the opposite sex.

4 **Hormones** bring about the changes that take place during puberty and adolescence.

5 **Sperm** are produced in the two **testes** of a man. When sperm are released they are mixed with special fluids which nourish the sperm and give them something to swim in.

6 **Eggs** are stored in the two **ovaries** of a woman. Usually only one egg is released from an ovary each month. The ovaries usually take it in turns to release an egg.

7 At the time of egg release, **ovulation**, the lining of the uterus is thick and has a rich blood supply. If the egg is not fertilised it breaks down and is lost. The lining of the uterus breaks down also after a time. This is lost as the monthly bleeding, period or **menstruation**.

8 Sperm released during sexual intercourse swim into the uterus and up the oviducts towards the ovaries. If an egg is present, moving down one of the oviducts, it will be met by the incoming sperm. The nucleus in the one successful sperm fuses with the nucleus already present in the egg. This is called **fertilisation**.

9 The fertilised egg divides to form a ball of cells called the **embryo**. The embryo continues to develop, lodged in the lining of the uterus for about thirty-eight weeks. The embryo is linked to its mother by an umbilical cord and a placenta.

10 The **placenta** allows the exchange of vital materials to take place between the mother's and the embryo's blood. The two blood systems are brought close together but are separated by membranes.

*Secondary sexual characteristics of humans*

| males | females |
|---|---|
| bodies become more muscular, voice breaks | breasts enlarge, hips widen |
| hair grows on face, chest and armpits | hair grows in armpits |
| pubic hair grows | pubic hair grows |
| sperm produced | eggs released, periods start |

*The menstrual cycle*

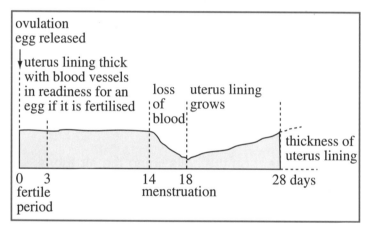

*Fertilisation of an egg*

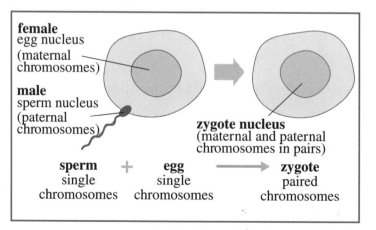

# Quick Questions

1 Name the hormone responsible for the development of secondary sexual characteristics in boys.

2 Describe two secondary sexual characteristics shown by girls.

3 What is the function of the fluid part of semen?

4 What is meant by the term ovulation?

5 Blood is lost from the vagina during menstruation. Where does this blood come from?

6 What is the function of the vas deferens?

7 List the structures in the female reproductive system through which sperm travel when they are released into the vagina.

8 In which part of the female reproductive system does fertilisation normally take place?

9 What is meant by the term fertilisation?

10 How does a human embryo receive nutrients?

## What you need to know

1  Air enters and leaves the body through the nose and mouth. The air passes into and out of the lungs along the **trachea** (windpipe). The trachea divides into two **bronchi** to carry air to and from the two lungs. The air tubes (bronchioles) divide many times to form the bronchial tree. Air sacs known as **alveoli** are found at the end of each of the fine tubes.

2  The internal surface of the bronchial tree is very large. The surface is thin, moist and has a very good blood supply. Together, these features make it a very efficient **gas exchange** surface.

3  Blood **capillaries** lie close to the air sacs. Blood arrives at the exchange surface in capillaries of the **pulmonary artery** and leaves in capillaries of the **pulmonary vein**.

4  **Oxygen** diffuses from the air sacs into the blood. **Carbon dioxide** diffuses out of the blood into the air sacs.

5  Tobacco smoke contains many chemicals. Tars and carbon monoxide in particular affect the lung structure and gas exchange.

6  Tars paralyse cilia (hair-like structures) present on the cells lining the air tubes. Paralysed cilia are unable to move mucus and bacteria out of the air passages. Bronchitis may result. Tars also damage the walls of the alveoli reducing the surface area for gas exchange.

7  Carbon monoxide combines permanently with haemoglobin to form carboxyhaemoglobin. Haemoglobin normally carries oxygen. This can mean that a smoker's blood carries up to 15% less oxygen than that of a non-smoker.

8  Cells use food as a fuel.
Food is oxidised in cells by a process known as **aerobic respiration**.
Energy is released during this process.

9  Carbon dioxide and water are produced as wastes when glucose is oxidised during aerobic respiration.

10 Aerobic respiration is summarised in the following word equation:

**glucose + oxygen → carbon dioxide + water + energy**

*Human respiratory pathway*

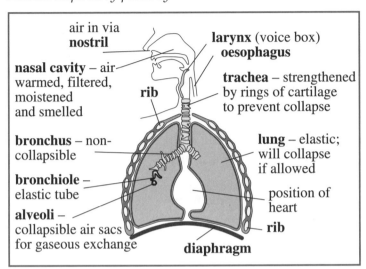

air in via **nostril**

**nasal cavity** – air warmed, filtered, moistened and smelled

**rib**

**bronchus** – non-collapsible

**bronchiole** – elastic tube

**alveoli** – collapsible air sacs for gaseous exchange

**larynx** (voice box)
**oesophagus**

**trachea** – strengthened by rings of cartilage to prevent collapse

**lung** – elastic; will collapse if allowed

position of heart

**rib**

**diaphragm**

*The blood supply to air sacs*

*Detailed section of one air sac*

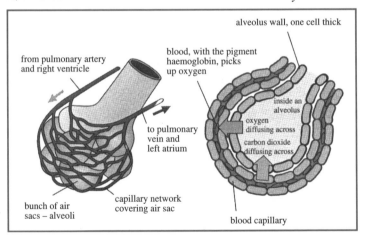

from pulmonary artery and right ventricle

to pulmonary vein and left atrium

bunch of air sacs – alveoli

capillary network covering air sac

alveolus wall, one cell thick

blood, with the pigment haemoglobin, picks up oxygen

inside an alveolus

oxygen diffusing across

carbon dioxide diffusing across

blood capillary

## Key concept

Oxyhaemoglobin is formed when oxygen combines with haemoglobin in a red blood cell. It breaks down readily to release oxygen.

Carboxyhaemoglobin is formed when carbon monoxide combines with haemoglobin. It does not break down.

## Quick Questions

1 List, in order, the structures through which air passes from the atmosphere to the air sacs.

2 List four features of the lung that make it an efficient gas-exchange surface.

3 Which blood vessel carries oxygenated blood away from a lung?

4 How do gases enter and leave the blood in the capillaries close to the air sacs?

5 What function do cilia associated with the bronchi carry out in a healthy individual?

6 Which chemicals present in tobacco smoke affect the function of the cilia in the air passages of humans?

7 What is the function of haemoglobin?

8 What is carboxyhaemoglobin?

9 Which is the most common food chemical respired aerobically?

10 Write out the word equation for aerobic respiration.

## What you need to know

1  All **drugs** affect the way the brain and nervous system work.

2  Some drugs occur naturally as products of living things. **Synthetic drugs** are chemicals made by man to copy the effects of naturally occurring drugs.

3  **Organic solvents** are chemicals used to dissolve substances, e.g. paint or glue, that are insoluble in water.

4  Drugs and solvents can cause physical damage to the human body as well as personal and social problems, if they are not used properly.

| substance | possible long term effects |
|-----------|----------------------------|
| alcohol | liver damage<br>brain damage |
| nicotine | bronchitis<br>increased risk of cancer |
| solvents | brain damage<br>liver damage<br>kidney damage<br>heart damage |

5  Bacteria and viruses are **microorganisms**. Some of them cause disease. Disease-causing microorganisms are known as **pathogens**.

6  **Bacteria** and **viruses** that cause disease are **parasites**.

| microorganism | disease | symptom |
|---------------|---------|---------|
| bacterium | e.g. cholera | severe diarrhoea |
| virus | e.g. influenza | headache, sore throat, fever |

7 Unless it is punctured, e.g. by a cut, the skin keeps pathogens out.

8 **White blood cells** try to destroy any pathogens that do get in.

9 **Medicines**, including drugs, can be used to treat or prevent disease.

10 **Immunisation** can be used to help the human body in its fight against a pathogen. **Vaccines** contain compounds that encourage the body's natural defence system to work or give immediate protection if the person has a dangerous infection.

---

### Key concept

- Alcohol, caffeine and tobacco (nicotine) are drugs.
- Tea, coffee, cola and cocoa contain caffeine.
- A parasite is an organism that lives in or on another living organism (its host) from which it gains nutrients at its host's expense.
- Some white blood cells protect the body by feeding on bacterial cells. Others release chemicals into the blood stream in an attempt to make the bacteria ineffective.
- Antibiotics are ineffective against viruses.

---

## Quick Questions

1 What is the difference between natural and synthetic drugs?

2 Which drug is found in coffee, tea and cola?

3 Name three products found in the home that contain organic solvents.

4 Suggest two social problems that can arise from alcohol abuse.

5 What is meant by the term pathogen?

6 Name a disease caused by a virus and a disease caused by a bacterium.

7 Why is it important to clean a cut and keep it covered?

8 What part do white blood cells play in the control of disease?

9 Name an antibiotic.

10 What does immunisation do?

# What you need to know

**1**  Green plants make their own food by a process known as **photosynthesis**.

**2**  Photosynthesis produces **glucose** and, at the same time, **oxygen** which is given off as a waste product.

**3**  A plant uses glucose to make other compounds, thus allowing it to grow.

**4**  A plant uses some of the oxygen it makes for its own aerobic respiration. The rest, released into the atmosphere, is available for other living things to use.

**5**  **Carbon dioxide** and **water** are the raw materials a plant needs to photosynthesise. **Light** provides the energy needed to make photosynthesis work.

**6**  Cells that can photosynthesise contain structures called **chloroplasts**. Chloroplasts contain chlorophyll. This is a green pigment that absorbs light.

**7**  The following word equation summarises photosynthesis.

Light

Carbon dioxide + Water  ⟹  Glucose + Oxygen

Chlorophyll

*Leaf structure*

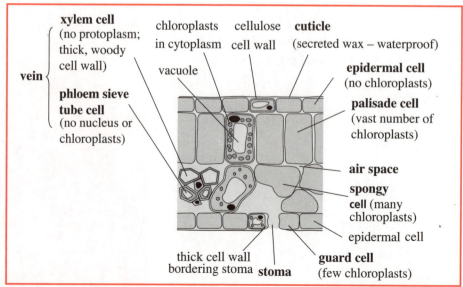

**xylem cell** (no protoplasm; thick, woody cell wall)

chloroplasts in cytoplasm

cellulose cell wall

**cuticle** (secreted wax – waterproof)

vacuole

**vein** {

**phloem sieve tube cell** (no nucleus or chloroplasts)

**epidermal cell** (no chloroplasts)

**palisade cell** (vast number of chloroplasts)

**air space**

**spongy cell** (many chloroplasts)

epidermal cell

thick cell wall bordering stoma  **stoma**

**guard cell** (few chloroplasts)

8   Plants get the elements carbon, hydrogen and oxygen from carbon dioxide and water. They need nitrogen and a variety of other elements for healthy growth.

9   **Nitrogen** is absorbed from the soil mainly in the form of nitrate ions. The soil provides other elements too, e.g. iron and magnesium.

10  Young, growing roots have surface cells adapted for absorption. These are called **root hair cells**. Together, the root hair cells provide a very large surface area to absorb water and mineral salts from the soil.

*Root hair cell*

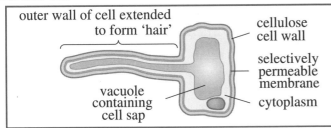

## Key concept

The table shows how different mineral nutrients are used in a plant.

| mineral nutrient | use in plant |
| --- | --- |
| nitrogen sulphur phosphorus potassium | important in the synthesis of protoplasm |
| calcium | important in cell division |
| magnesium iron | important in the synthesis of chlorophyll |

1   What are the raw materials for photosynthesis?

2   Name the carbohydrate produced by photosynthesis.

3   Why is the oxygen produced by photosynthesis important?

4   What is the source of the energy that powers photosynthesis?

5   What is the function of chlorophyll?

6   Which cells in the leaf have the most chloroplasts?

7   Write out a word equation to summarise photosynthesis.

8   In what form does most nitrogen enter a plant?

9   Why do plants need magnesium to remain healthy?

10  How are root hair cells adapted to make them efficient at absorbing water and mineral salts?

# What you need to know

**1**  The sexual reproductive structures of flowering plants are found in their flowers.

**2**  Flowers are built up from four basic structures. These are **sepals**, **petals**, **stamens** and **carpels**.

**3**  Sepals protect the other parts inside a flower bud. Petals are often coloured to attract pollinators. Stamens are the male sex organs. Carpels are the female sex organs.

**4**  A stamen produces **pollen** (containing male nuclei). Carpels produce one or more **egg cells** (each containing a female nucleus).

**5**  **Pollination** is the transfer of pollen from a stamen to a carpel. Different flowers show a variety of adaptations to encourage successful pollination.

**6**  Some plants are insect-pollinated, some are wind pollinated, others employ different agents, e.g. birds or monkeys.

**7**  A pollen grain delivers male gametes to the ovule inside the ovary of a carpel, by producing a pollen tube. **Fertilisation** takes place when the male nuclei fuse with female nuclei present in the ovule.

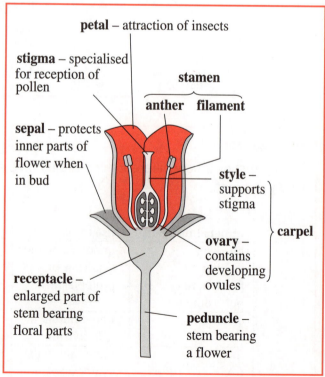

**8**  The fertilised ovule forms a **seed** inside the ovary. The ovary then undergoes changes to become a **fruit**.

**9**  The fruits of different flowers show a variety of adaptations to encourage the dispersal of the seed or seeds they contain.

**10**  Successfully dispersed seeds germinate to produce new plants.

*Vertical section through a flower*

## Key concept

The table shows how the parts of insect- and wind-pollinated flowers differ.

| flower part | insect pollinated | wind pollinated |
|---|---|---|
| petals | large, colourful | small, inconspicuous |
| stamens | short filaments | long filaments |
| anthers | inside flower | hang outside flower |
| stigmas | inside flower | feathery, hang outside flower |

*The diagram shows how the male nuclei in a pollen grain are delivered to an ovule deep inside the carpel.*

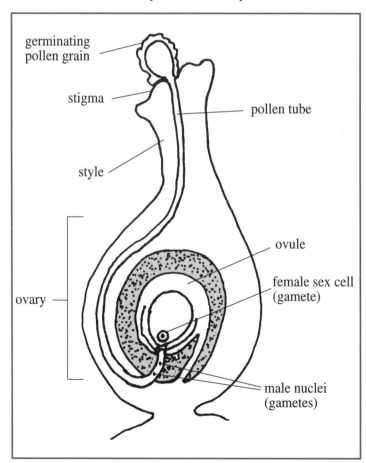

germinating pollen grain

stigma

pollen tube

style

ovary

ovule

female sex cell (gamete)

male nuclei (gametes)

## Quick Questions

1 What is the function of the sepals?

2 Name the male and female sex organs of a flowering plant.

3 What is the function of pollen grains?

4 How are the petals of many species of flowering plants adapted for their function in sexual reproduction?

5 What is meant by the term pollination?

6 How do the stamens of wind-pollinated flowers differ from those of insect-pollinated ones?

7 Where does fertilisation take place in flowering plants?

8 What happens to the ovule after fertilisation?

9 What forms the fruit of a flowering plant?

10 What environmental factors are required for germination of seeds?

**Variation, classification and inheritance**

# What you need to know

1. Living things show differences that identify them as different species or different members of the same species. They show **variation**.

2. All human beings have particular features that enable us to identify them as human beings and a package of variations that are peculiar to them. These are **genetic variations**, inherited from their parents.

| cause of variation | characteristic |
|---|---|
| genetic, affected by environment | e.g. body mass |
| genetic | e.g. eye colour |

3. Some variation is a result of **environmental causes**. For example, an individual human being may have inherited the potential to grow to a particular size. That potential may not be achieved, perhaps, because of lack of food.

4. Living things can be observed and their features recorded to construct a **key**. Keys often employ a series of questions that require a 'yes' or a 'no' answer. This allows grouping of similar organisms together. If an organism shows a particular feature it goes into one group, if it does not then it goes into the other group. Keys are useful in identification.

5. To start with, all living things are formally classified by placing them in a particular **Kingdom**. All the members of a particular Kingdom (of which there are five) will have some, particular features in common. A Kingdom is subdivided into groups called **Phyla** (singular Phylum). These are then progressively subdivided into **Classes**, **Orders**, **Families**, **Genera** (singular Genus) and finally **Species**.

6. Each major group is called a **taxon**. It is accepted practice to use a capital, initial letter for a genus and a small initial letter for the specific name, e.g. *Homo sapiens*.

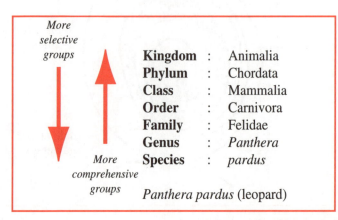

*More selective groups*

*More comprehensive groups*

| Kingdom | : | Animalia |
|---|---|---|
| Phylum | : | Chordata |
| Class | : | Mammalia |
| Order | : | Carnivora |
| Family | : | Felidae |
| Genus | : | *Panthera* |
| Species | : | *pardus* |

*Panthera pardus* (leopard)

*Taxonomic hierarchy for leopard*

18

**7** Human beings are classified as follows:

| Group | Human |
|-------|-------|
| Kingdom | Animal |
| Phylum | Chordate |
| Class | Mammal |
| Order | Primate |
| Family | Hominid |
| Genus | *Homo* |
| Species | *sapiens* |

**8** Man uses **selective breeding** to improve livestock and crop plants. An animal or plant with the desired characteristic can be crossed with another member of the same species having a different useful characteristic. This is done in the hope that these characteristics will show up together in some of the offspring. The 'special' offspring can be selected as parents for the next generation. Repeated crosses of this kind may lead to the establishment of an inbred line showing the 'selected characteristics'.

**9** Chickens have been selectively bred for rapid weight gain.

**10** Wheat varieties have been selectively bred for resistance to fungal disease.

1 Name two sources of variation in human beings.

2 Give an example of variation for each of the sources named in 1 above.

3 What determines the following human features:
Body mass
Eye colour
Number of fingers?

4 Name three different Kingdoms of living things.

5 List the following classification groups in the correct order:
Class/Family/Genus/Kingdom/Order/Phylum/Species.

6 What is wrong with the following specific name: *hippopotamus Amphibius*?

7 Write out the full classification for a human being.

8 What does the term 'selective breeding' mean?

9 Crop plants have been selectively bred to improve their performance. Name one example.

10 Chickens have been bred to show rapid weight gain. Suggest one other way that they might be improved to be more profitable.

# What you need to know

**1** When you visit a particular type of **habitat**, e.g. a freshwater pond or deciduous woodland, anywhere in the UK, you find the particular group of plants and animals you expect to be there. This is because each species of plant or animal can live only in a certain set of environmental conditions.

| habitat | organism | features that enable survival in extreme conditions |
|---|---|---|
| arctic | e.g. polar bear | large size, fur<br>thick layer of body fat<br>hibernation |
| desert | e.g. cactus | deep or wide spread root systems<br>very small leaves, or leaves<br>    reduced to spines<br>swollen stems<br>photosynthetic stems |

**2** Different types of habitat support different populations of plants and animals.

**3** Habitats differ in terms of the type of soil, daily and seasonal changes in temperature, light intensity, wind strength and rainfall and in the populations of plants and animals that live there.

**4** Some organisms are **adapted** to survive daily and seasonal changes in their habitats, e.g. temperature and water availability.

**5** All living things need space and food to live. All the members of a particular species will need the same things from their habitat. They have to compete with each other for those resources and this will limit the number of members of that species that can survive in that habitat.

**6** **Predators** also play a part in determining the size of populations of prey animals. Grazing animals do the same to the plant populations they feed on.

**7** Organisms that compete successfully for the resources found in a habitat are more likely to reproduce successfully. Their offspring are more likely to survive than those of competitively weak parents.

**8** A **food chain** represents the sequence of organisms involved in a feeding relationship. For example:
producer (plant) $\rightarrow$ herbivore (plant eater) $\rightarrow$ carnivore (animal eater).

| term | meaning |
|------|---------|
| carnivore | an animal that feeds on other animals |
| herbivore | an animal that feeds exclusively on plants |
| omnivore | an animal that feeds on plants and animals |
| consumer | an organism that feeds on ready-made food, i.e. other organisms |
| predator | a carnivore that kills and eats other animals |
| prey | an animal that forms the food of a predator |

The size of the population at each stage in the food chain can be represented graphically. The graph produced is called a **pyramid of numbers**.

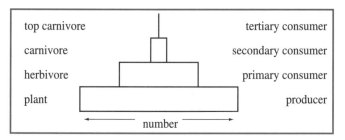

9   **Food webs** are interconnected food chains. Links between the chains occur where a producer or consumer can be eaten by more than one consumer.

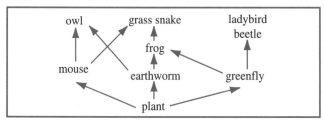

10  As a general rule populations of organisms decrease in size the further along the food chain they occur. This means that toxic (poisonous) materials introduced early in the food chain are likely to accumulate, increasing in concentration as they pass from one link in the chain to the next.

1   Why do different types of habitat support different populations of animals and plants?

2   Name three climatic factors that affect a habitat.

3   Polar bears are adapted to survive in a very cold climate. List three features that enable them to survive in the Arctic.

4   Cacti are adapted to survive in deserts. Give two features shown by many cacti that enable them to survive in deserts.

5   What does the term 'competition' mean when it's used in biology?

6   Name a predator and its usual prey.

7   Write out a food chain where Man is the last consumer.

8   Why are plants called 'producers' in food chains?

9   How do the diets of a herbivore and a carnivore differ?

10  How can poisons used on weeds kill carnivorous birds?

# What you need to know

**1**   There are three states of matter – **solid**, **liquid** and **gas**.

**2**   The change of state from solid to liquid is called **melting** and takes place at the **melting point**. During melting energy is taken in from the surroundings.

**3**   The change of state from liquid to gas happens by a process of **evaporation** or **boiling**. Evaporation takes place at all temperatures and boiling takes place at the **boiling point**. The change of state from liquid to gas requires energy to be taken in.

**4**   The change of state from liquid to solid is called **freezing** and takes place at the **freezing point**. When freezing takes place energy is given out to the surroundings.

**5**   The change of state from gas to liquid is called **condensation**. When condensing takes place energy is given out to the surroundings.

**6**   In a solid the particles are usually close together, regularly arranged and the movement is limited to vibrations.

**7**   In a liquid the particles are still close together but there is no regular arrangement. The particles move more freely but their movement is still limited.

**8**   In a gas the particles are free to move. Their movement is in all directions and without any pattern (random motion).

## Key concepts

The table shows the differences in properties between solids, liquids and gases.

| state | density | ease of squeezing | ease of flow | keeps its volume? | keeps its shape? |
|-------|---------|-------------------|--------------|-------------------|------------------|
| solid | high | hard | does not pour * | yes | yes |
| liquid | medium | hard | pours | yes | no – it takes shape of the bottom of container |
| gas | low | easy | pours** | no – changes its volume | no – it takes up the volume of the container |

\*     It is possible to pour a solid when it is in the form of a powder. Many of the properties of a powder resemble those of a liquid.

\*\*    It is possible to pour some denser gases such as carbon dioxide or bromine vapour.

**9** **Pressure** is caused by collisions between particles and the walls of their container. The more collisions between the particles and the walls of the container, the higher the pressure.

**10** The movement of particles to fill all of the available space is called **diffusion**. Diffusion occurs faster in gases than in solids or liquids.

---

**Examiner's Tips**

Most pupils are able to draw diagrams of particles in a solid and a gas. They find difficulty drawing the diagram for a liquid. Remember the particles must be arranged irregularly and at least two-thirds of them must be touching to score a mark.

It is easier to draw diagrams of this type if the particles you draw are not too small or too large. You should make sure your diagram for a liquid or solid contains more than about 12 particles.

---

*The diffusion of bromine vapour*

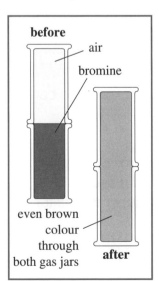

before

air

bromine

even brown colour through both gas jars

**after**

*The arrangement of particles in solids liquids and gases*

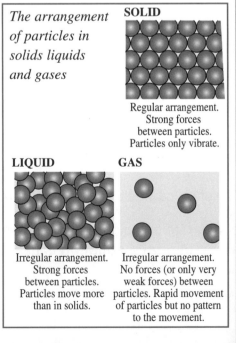

**SOLID**

Regular arrangement. Strong forces between particles. Particles only vibrate.

**LIQUID**

Irregular arrangement. Strong forces between particles. Particles move more than in solids.

**GAS**

Irregular arrangement. No forces (or only very weak forces) between particles. Rapid movement of particles but no pattern to the movement.

## Quick Questions

1 In what state, at room temperature and atmospheric pressure, is water?

2 What name is given to the solid form of water?

3 What is the melting point of ice and the freezing point of water?

4 What is the boiling point of water at atmospheric pressure?

5 Why does the pressure of a gas increase when its volume is decreased?

6 Why does the pressure of a gas increase when a gas is heated?

7 What name is given to the change of state when solid carbon dioxide turns directly to carbon dioxide gas?

8 When a bottle of perfume is opened, the smell quickly spreads throughout the room. What name is given to the process causing this?

9 Why does a substance in the form of a solid usually have a higher density than the same substance in the form of a liquid? Use your knowledge of particles.

10 Write down the name of a solid that is less dense than the liquid from which it is formed.

23

**Elements, mixtures and compounds**

## What you need to know

1 An **element** is a pure substance that cannot be split up into simpler substances.

2 There are just over 100 elements that make up all of the matter. Elements are shown in the periodic table. Each element can be represented by a **symbol**, e.g. C for carbon, Ca for calcium and Cu for copper.

3 All elements are made up of **atoms**. Carbon is made up only of carbon atoms and copper is made only of copper atoms.

4 All atoms of the same element contain the same number of particles called **protons**.

5 Elements **combine** together in chemical reactions to form compounds. For example, two hydrogen atoms combine with one oxygen atom to form a **compound** called water.

6 Compounds have properties which are different from the elements which make them up. The elements are in fixed proportions. Compunds can be represented by a formula, e.g. $H_2O$.

*The diagrams summarise the changes that take place when iron and sulphur are mixed and then combined to form a compound called iron(II) sulphide.*
*This compound has the formula FeS.*
*This tells us that one iron atom combines with one sulphur atom.*

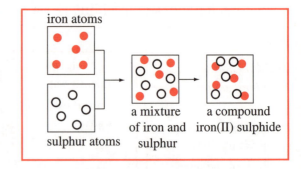

7 In a mixture, e.g. air, the substances that make it up are not combined and can be separated.

8 A mixture of sand and salt solution can be separated by **filtration**.

9 **Distillation** can be used to separate a liquid from impurities that dissolve in it, e.g. water from salt solution. **Fractional distillation** is used to separate mixtures of liquids with different boiling points.

**10 Chromatography** is used to separate mixtures of coloured dyes in solution.

---

### Key concepts

When elements combine to form a compound, atoms of the elements join together in fixed numbers. Often an energy change accompanies compound formation.

Understanding how atoms combine to form compounds is an important idea. The elements can be separated easily in a mixture but not in a compound.

---

*The separation of a solid from a solution by filtration*

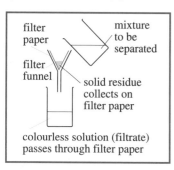

*The separation of a liquid by distillation*

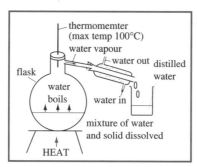

*The separation of a mixture of liquids by fractional distillation*

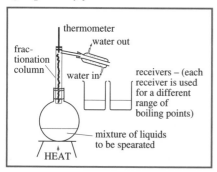

*The process of chromatography*

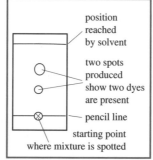

## Quick Questions

1   What name is given to pure substances that cannot be split up into simpler substances?

2   Which one of the substances in the list is an element?
    **air**
    **brass**
    **distilled water**
    **oxygen**
    **sea water**

3   How could you separate a mixture of iron and sulphur?

4   Write down one way a mixture of hydrogen and oxygen is different from the compound hydrogen oxide (water).

5   Write down the names of the two elements in copper oxide.

6   Which method could be used to separate some small pieces of glass from water?

7   Which method could be used to show that an orange squash contains two dyes?

8   Which method could be used to separate ethanol (boiling point 78°C) from water (boiling point 100°C)?

9   Sulphuric acid has a formula $H_2SO_4$. Write down the names of the three elements in sulphuric acid.

10  In the compound aluminium iodide, one aluminium combines with three iodine atoms. The symbols for aluminium and iodine are Al and I. Write down the formula of aluminium iodide.

# What you need to know

1   Elements can be divided into two groups – metals and non-metals.

2   Most elements (apart from helium) ending in -ium are metals. Some elements not ending in -ium are also metals, e.g. copper and iron.

3   Most metallic elements are shiny solids at room temperature.

4   Most metallic elements are good conductors of heat and electricity.

5   A few metallic elements, e.g. iron, cobalt and nickel, are strongly magnetic.

6   Non-metallic elements can be solids or liquids but many are gases at room temperature and pressure.

7   Most non-metallic elements are poor conductors of heat and electrical energy.

8   Physical properties can be used to classify elements as metallic or non-metallic. However, use of physical properties alone can lead to mistakes. For example, graphite, a form of the non-metal carbon, is a good conductor of electricity.

| metals | non-metals |
|---|---|
| solid at room temperature | solid, liquid or gas at room temperature |
| shiny | dull |
| conduct heat and electricity | do not conduct electricity |
| can be beaten into a thin sheet (it is malleable) or drawn into a wire (it is ductile) | easily broken |
| sometimes magnetic | never magnetic |

**Key concepts**

- Metals form neutral or alkaline oxides. Non-metals form acidic oxides.
- Elements can be grouped as metals or non-metals using their physical or chemical properties.

**9** Metals burn in oxygen (or air) to form oxides. Metal oxides have pH values of 7 or above (neutral or alkaline).

**10** Non-metals burn in oxygen (or air) to form oxides. Non-metal oxides have pH values below 7 (acidic).

*Apparatus used to burn elements in oxygen*

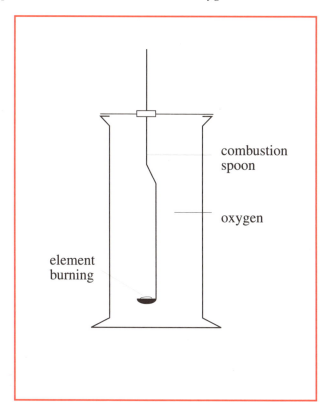

combustion spoon

oxygen

element burning

## Quick Questions

**1** Name a metal that is liquid at room temperature.

**2** Which element in the list is a metal?
**bromine**        **iodine**
**magnesium**     **sulphur**

**3** Name a non-metal that is liquid at room temperature.

**4** Many non-metals are gases at room temperature and atmospheric pressure. Which element in the list is a gaseous non-metal?
**hydrogen**
**iodine**
**phosphorus**
**sulphur**

**5** Most metallic elements are silvery in colour. Which metallic element is not grey or silver in colour?
**aluminium**
**copper**
**iron**
**lead**
**mercury**

**6** An element burns in oxygen to form a residue. What is this residue called?

**7** An element burns in oxygen to form a residue with a pH value of 2. Is the element a metal or a non-metal?

**8** An element burns in oxygen to form a residue with a pH value of 10. Is the element a metal or a non-metal?

**9** An element burns in oxygen to form a residue with a pH value of 7. Is the element a metal or a non-metal?

**10** Metals are said to be malleable and ductile. What do these words mean?

# What you need to know

**1** A physical change can be easily reversed. For example, melting ice or dissolving salt in water.

**2** When a physical change takes place, there is no change in total mass.

**3** Different substances change state at different temperatures.

**4** A substance that is dissolved is called a **solute**. The substance that does the dissolving is called the **solvent**. The mixture is called a **solution**. For example, when salt dissolves in water, salt is the solute, water is the solvent and the mixture is called a salt solution.

**5** The maximum mass of solute that can be dissolved in 100 g of water at a particular temperature is called the **solubility** of the solute. The solubilities of different solutes at the same temperature are very different.

**6** The solution that contains the maximum mass of solute dissolved in a given mass of solvent at a particular temperature is called a **saturated solution**.

**7** The solubility of the same solute in different solvents at the same temperature varies. For example, salt dissolves well in water but very little in petrol.

**8** The solubility of a solid solute usually increases with increasing temperature. An exception to this is sodium chloride which has approximately the same solubility at all temperatures.

**9** Gaps are left between lengths of railway track to allow for the track to expand when temperature rises. Without these, the tremendous forces produced would buckle the railway track. The forces that accompany expansion and contraction are great.

**10** Energy changes accompany changes of state (see page 22).

*Solubility graphs of sodium chloride, potassium nitrate, copper sulphate*

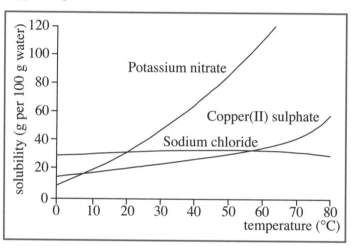

## Quick Questions

Iodine dissolves in ethanol to form a liquid that is sometimes called tincture of iodine.

1   Which substance is the solvent?

2   Which substance is the solution?

3   Which substance is the solute?

4   A sample of salt weighing 10 g is dissolved in 100 g of water. What is the mass of the resulting solution?

Calcium carbonate reacts with hydrochloric acid in a test tube to produce bubbles of carbon dioxide gas and leave colourless calcium chloride solution.

5   Why is it wrong to write that 'the calcium carbonate dissolves'?

6   Would the mass of the products in the test tube be the same, less or more at the end of the process?

7   The solubility of a solute is 150 g at 80° C and 20 g at 20° C.
    What would be the result of cooling a saturated solution (containing 100 g of water) from 80° C to 20° C?

8   A metal pipe carrying cold water can break in very cold weather but a similar pipe carrying gas does not. Why?

9   Look at the solubility curves.
    Which substance is most soluble at 10° C?

10  Which substance is most soluble at 60° C?

# What you need to know

**1** Rocks can be broken down, or **weathered**, by the action of water. Water gets into cracks in the rock. When the water freezes, it expands as the ice forms. The tremendous forces produced push the rock apart.

**2** Rocks can also be broken down by processes involving movement. These processes, called **erosion**, may include chemical reactions.

**3** Rocks can be broken down by weathering and erosion to produce smaller pieces called sediments.

**4** Sediments can be **transported** in rivers and streams and become **deposited** when the speed of the water decreases.

**5** Rock sediments build up in layers and with compression and cementation (sticking together) can produce new rocks called **sedimentary rocks**.

**6** The effects of high temperature and high pressure on existing sedimentary rocks produces **metamorphic rocks**.

**7** Existing rocks are melting all the time and returning to the **magma**.

**8** When the magma cools and crystallises new crystalline rocks called **igneous rocks** are formed.

**9** The recycling of existing rocks to form new rocks takes place over millions of years and is summarised in the **rock cycle**.

**10** The remains of plants and animals (called **fossils**) in rocks can be used to date rocks. Fossils are found in sedimentary rocks and sometimes in metamorphic rocks but never in igneous rocks.

## Weathering of rocks

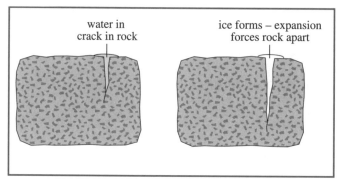

water in crack in rock

ice forms – expansion forces rock apart

## Key concepts

- Rocks are recycled in the rock cycle. Existing rocks return to the magma and new rocks are formed to replace them. The rock cycle can be compared to the processes involved in recycling glass bottles to form new bottles.
- There are three types of rock – sedimentary, metamorphic and igneous. A rock is classified as one of these types according to how it was made.

## Rock cycle

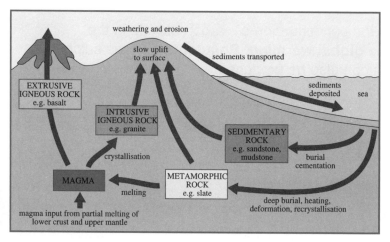

weathering and erosion

slow uplift to surface

sediments transported

sediments deposited    sea

EXTRUSIVE IGNEOUS ROCK e.g. basalt

INTRUSIVE IGNEOUS ROCK e.g. granite

SEDIMENTARY ROCK e.g. sandstone, mudstone

burial cementation

crystallisation

MAGMA

melting

METAMORPHIC ROCK e.g. slate

deep burial, heating, deformation, recrystallisation

magma input from partial melting of lower crust and upper mantle

# Quick Questions

Here is a list of rocks

**chalk**
**granite**
**limestone**
**marble**

1 Which rock is an igneous rock?

2 Which rock is a metamorphic rock?

3 Which two rocks are sedimentary rocks?

4 Which rock does not contain calcium carbonate?

5 Which rock can never contain fossils?

6 The diagram below shows a magnified drawing of a piece of sandstone. Why do the grains not have any sharp edges?

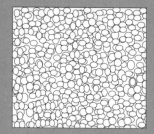

7 A cliff is made up of many different layers of sedimentary rocks. Which rock is the oldest?

8 Igneous rocks contain crystals. A sample of rock contains large crystals. What does this tell us about how it was formed?

9 Bricks are made by baking clay. Which type of rock is formed in a similar way to the way bricks are made?

10 Name two useful materials made from rocks.

# What you need to know

1   The mass of the reactants in a chemical reaction is the same as the mass of the products, providing no materials are lost or gained.

2   Almost all materials are made by chemical reactions.

3   A chemical reaction can be summarised by a word equation.
    For example:
    magnesium  +  oxygen  →  magnesium oxide.

4   There are different types of reaction. **Oxidation** is a reaction where oxygen is gained and **reduction** is a reaction where oxygen is lost.

5   **Combustion** is the reaction of a substance with oxygen, usually accompanied by an energy change. Combustion reactions are examples of **oxidation** reactions.

6   **Decomposition** is the splitting up of a compound. This can be by heating (**thermal**), with a catalyst (**catalytic**) and by electricity (**electrolytic**).

7   Some chemical reactions produce useful materials, e.g. reactions producing metals from metal oxides.

8   Some chemical reactions are not useful, e.g. rusting of iron or the spoiling food.

9   It is possible to control and use the energy released in chemical reactions. For example, the energy from burning fuels can be used to produce electricity.

10  Burning fossil fuels increases the concentration of carbon dioxide in the atmosphere. This can increase **global warming**. **Pollutants** such as sulphur dioxide and oxides of nitrogen can also be produced.

## Key concepts

- The mass of **all** the reactants equals the mass of **all** the products.
- Chemical reactions can be represented by equations. Word equations are summaries of reactions. Reactants are on the left-hand side of equations and products on the right.
- Some chemical reactions are useful and some are not.

*The reaction of hydrogen with lead(II) oxide. The diagram shows the apparatus used for this reaction.*

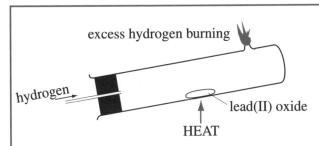

The word equation for the reaction is:

lead(II) oxide + hydrogen → lead + hydrogen oxide.

Lead(II) oxide is reduced – loses oxygen.
Hydrogen is oxidised – gains oxygen.

## Quick Questions

Joseph Priestley produced oxygen by heating mercury(II) oxide. The other product was mercury.

1 Write a word equation for this reaction.

2 What type of reaction is this?

Molten lead(II) bromide is split up by passing electricity through it. One product is lead.

3 Write a word equation for this reaction.

4 What type of reaction is this?

5 A reaction producing energy is described as exothermic and one needing energy as endothermic. Is the splitting up of lead(II) bromide exothermic or endothermic?

Zinc can be made by heating zinc oxide with carbon. The other product is carbon monoxide.

6 Write a word equation for this reaction.

7 Is the zinc oxide oxidised or reduced in this reaction?

8 Is the carbon oxidised or reduced in this reaction?

9 This reaction is a redox reaction. What is the meaning of the term redox?

10 Why are more natural gas power stations being built and fewer coal power stations?

# What you need to know

**1** Most metals react with air to form oxides, water to form hydroxides or oxides and dilute acids to form hydrogen gas.

**2** Different metals react with air, water and dilute acids at different rates.

**3** The reactivity series is a list of metals (or league table of metals) in order of reactivity. Metals at the top of the list are most reactive and metals at the bottom least reactive.

## Key concepts

The table summarises the reactions of some common metals with air (containing oxygen), water and dilute hydrochloric acid.

| metal | reaction with air | reaction with water | reaction with dilute hydrochloric acid |
|---|---|---|---|
| potassium | | reacts violently with cold water to produce hydrogen. This burns with a lilac flame. | violent reaction to produce hydrogen |
| sodium | | reacts quickly with cold water to produce hydrogen. Hydrogen does not ignite. | |
| calcium | burn in air or oxygen to form an oxide | reacts slowly with cold water to produce hydrogen | reacts with acid to produce a metal chloride and hydrogen reacts more slowly down the list |
| magnesium | | reacts very slowly with cold water, rapidly with steam | |
| zinc | | reacts fairly quickly with steam | |
| iron | | reacts only reversibly with steam | |
| lead | converted to oxide by heating | | very slow reaction to produce hydrogen |
| copper | in air or oxygen but do not burn | no reaction with water or steam | no reaction with dilute hydrochloric acid |
| silver | not affected by air or oxygen | | |

4   The method used to extract a metal from its ore depends upon the position of the metal in the reactivity series.

5   If a metal X is placed in a metal salt solution containing metal Y, a reaction will take place if X is more reactive than Y (i.e. higher in the reactivity series).

6   No reaction will take place in this type of reaction if X is less reactive than Y.

7   A reaction where one metal replaces a less reactive metal is called a displacement reaction.

8   The reactivity series can be used to make predictions about possible chemical reactions.

9   If a mixture of iron oxide and aluminium powder is heated, a displacement reaction takes place. The equation is:

iron oxide + aluminium → iron + aluminium oxide

This reaction is used to weld lengths of railway track together.

10  Metals high in the reactivity series form stable compounds which are difficult to split up.

---

**Examiner's Tip**

Many students try to remember the order of reactivity of metals. This is a waste of time. It will be given to you if you need to use it.

---

## Quick Questions

(Refer to the table on page 34 giving the metals in order of reactivity and their reactions with air, water and dilute hydrochloric acid.)

1   Which metal in the table is most reactive?

2   Which metal in the table is least reactive?

3   The table given does not include aluminium. Aluminium is more reactive than zinc and less reactive than magnesium. Where does it fit into the table?

4   Write the word equation for the reaction of zinc and dilute hydrochloric acid.

5   A piece of lead is dipped into zinc sulphate. Does a reaction take place?

When a piece of iron is put into blue copper(II) sulphate solution, the solution turns almost colourless and a brown solid forms on the iron.

6   What is the brown solid?

7   What name is given to this type of reaction?

8   Write a word equation for the reaction.

9   A metal reacts with lead(II) nitrate solution but not with zinc sulphate solution. Suggest a metal that would behave in this way.

10  The same gas is produced when metals react with water and with hydrochloric acid. Name this gas.

# What you need to know

1  **Acids** are compounds that contain the element hydrogen. This hydrogen can be replaced by a metal to form a **salt**.

2  The three common laboratory acids are hydrochloric acid, sulphuric acid and nitric acid.

3  A **base** is a metal oxide. A base that dissolves in water forms an **alkali**.

4  Three common alkalis are sodium hydroxide, potassium hydroxide and calcium hydroxide.

5  Acids and alkalis can be detected using indicators. **Litmus** turns red in an acid and blue in an alkali. **Universal indicator** gives the pH value.

6  Acids have a pH value of less than 7 and alkalis a pH value greater than 7. A neutral substance has a pH value of 7.

7  Acids react with metals, bases, alkalis and carbonates to form salts.

8  The reaction of an acid with an alkali is called **neutralisation**.

9  Examples of neutralisation include treatment of indigestion and curing the excess acidity of some soils.

10  Acids such as sulphuric acid and nitric acid can get into the atmosphere and can lead to corrosion of metals and chemical weathering of rocks.

*pH chart*

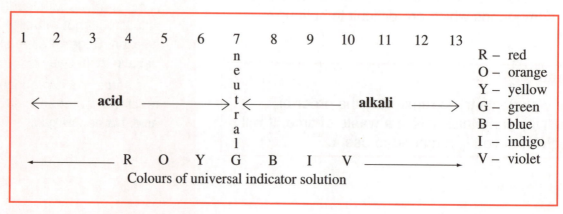

Colours of universal indicator solution

## Key concepts

- Neutralisation is the reaction of an acid with an alkali.
- Litmus turns red in acids and blue in alkalis.
- Universal indicator is used to detect the strength of acids and alkalis.

*The stages in making magnesium sulphate*

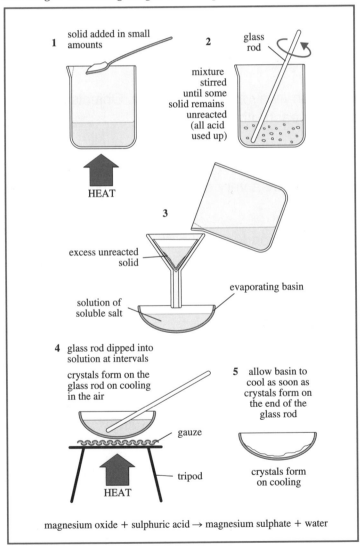

1 solid added in small amounts

2 glass rod

mixture stirred until some solid remains unreacted (all acid used up)

HEAT

3

excess unreacted solid

solution of soluble salt

evaporating basin

4 glass rod dipped into solution at intervals

crystals form on the glass rod on cooling in the air

5 allow basin to cool as soon as crystals form on the end of the glass rod

gauze

tripod

HEAT

crystals form on cooling

magnesium oxide + sulphuric acid → magnesium sulphate + water

## Quick Questions

1 Which element is present in all acids?

2 A solution has a pH value of 1. What does this mean?

3 A solution is added to neutralise a solution with a pH value of 1. This solution could have a pH value of

**2    4    7    10**

4 Sodium hydroxide is an alkali. Name the three elements in sodium hydroxide.

Excess calcium carbonate is added to 25 cm$^3$ of dilute hydrochloric acid.

5 Name the gas produced.

6 What is the final pH value of the mixture?

7 Why is lime (calcium hydroxide) added to some soils?

8 Why does a steel car body rust more quickly in an industrial city than in the countryside?

9 Why do indigestion tablets contain a weak alkali?

10 Which of the substances in the list is a salt?

**aluminium hydroxide**
**sodium hydroxide**
**ethanoic acid**
**potassium nitrate**

# What you need to know

1 Charge can pass easily through **conductors**, such as metals.

2 Charge cannot pass through **insulators**, such as polythene, rubber, nylon and plastics.

3 **Friction** is a force that opposes slipping and sliding. The friction forces that act when two objects are rubbed together cause electrons to move from one object to the other object.

4 **Electrons** are the outermost particles of **atoms**. They are negatively charged.

5 When an object gains electrons, it becomes negatively charged. The object that loses electrons becomes positively charged.

6 Objects with similar charges **repel** (push away from) each other. Objects with opposite charges **attract** (pull towards) each other.

7 Insulators keep their charge when they are charged by friction.

8 Unless they are separated from the Earth by a very good insulator, conductors easily lose their charge.

9 A flow of charge is an electric current. In a conductor, the charge is carried by electrons which can move freely through the conductor.

10 In a molten or dissolved electrolyte or an ionised gas, charge is carried by both positive ions and negative ions.

**Key concepts**

Remember:
- electro**N**s are **N**egatively charged;
- similar charges repel, opposite charges attract;
- the current in a metal is due to a flow of electrons from negative to positive.

*The diagrams show the attractive forces between a charged balloon and the duster used to charge it and the repulsive forces between two charged balloons.*

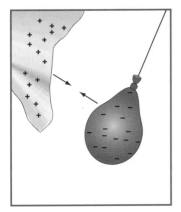 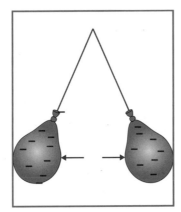

### Examiner's tip

When drawing the forces between charged objects, take care to draw one arrow on each object. The arrows must be separate. A common error is to draw the forces on two charged balloons like this:

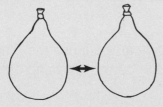

It is not clear which arrow acts on each balloon.

## Quick Questions

1. Name the force that opposes slipping and sliding.
2. Name the particles that are transferred when two objects rub together.
3. What is the sign of the charge on these particles?
4. Whereabouts in the atom are these particles situated?
5. How does an object become positively charged?
6. What type of force do two positively charged plastic rulers exert on each other?
7. What type of force do two negatively charged sheets of polythene exert on each other?
8. What type of force do a positively charged plastic ruler and a negatively charged sheet of polythene exert on each other?
9. Which particles pass through a metal when it is conducting electricity?
10. Which particles pass through a gas when it is conducting electricity?

# What you need to know

1  A **series circuit** has only one current path between the positive and negative terminals of the power supply.

2  A circuit where there is more than one current path is called a **parallel circuit**.

3  A **switch** placed anywhere in a series circuit affects all the components in the circuit. A switch in a parallel circuit affects only those components that are in the same current path.

4  **Current** is measured in amps using an ammeter.

5  The current in a series circuit is the same at all points in the circuit; an ammeter in a series circuit gives the same reading wherever it is placed.

6  The current that enters a component such as a lamp or a motor is equal to the current that leaves the component; lamps and other circuit components do not 'use up' any current.

7  The job of the current in a circuit is to transfer energy from the power supply to the lamps and other components.

8  The size of the current that passes in a series circuit depends on the power supply voltage (or number of cells in the battery) and the number of components in the circuit. Increasing the voltage increases the current, but increasing the number of components makes the current smaller because there is more resistance in the circuit.

9  In a **parallel circuit** the current splits and rejoins at the junctions. The total current that passes into a junction is equal to the current passing out of the junction.

10  The current is not the same at all points in a parallel circuit. An ammeter placed between the power supply and a junction measures the total current in the circuit. An ammeter placed in a branch of the circuit measures the current in that branch only.

*The diagrams show measurements of current in series and parallel circuits.*

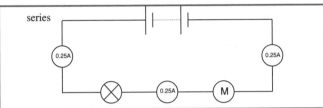

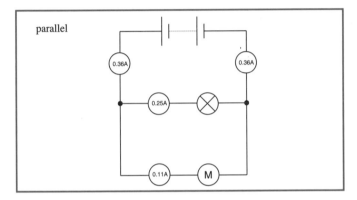

# Quick Questions

1   What is the unit of electric current?

2   Name the instrument used for measuring electric current.

3   What type of circuit has only one current path?

4   What type of circuit has more than one current path?

5   In which type of circuit is the current the same everywhere?

6   Complete the sentence:

    The current that enters a junction of a parallel circuit is _____ the sum of the currents that leave the junction.

7   The lamp in a torch is described as '2.5 V, 0.25 A'.
    How much current does the lamp use up?

8   A circuit consists of a motor, a lamp and a battery connected in parallel.
    The current in the motor is 0.50 A.
    The current in the lamp is 0.30 A.
    What is the value of the current in the battery?

9   A circuit consists of two identical lamps in series with a battery. The current in the first lamp is 0.25 A.
    Is the current in the second lamp less than 0.25 A, equal to 0.25 A or greater than 0.25 A?

10  A set of fairy lights uses 20 lamps in series with the mains supply.
    How many switches are needed to control all of them?

## What you need to know

1 The common magnetic materials are iron, steel and nickel.

2 Every magnet has its own **magnetic field**; this is the area around the magnet where it exerts a force on magnetic materials.

3 The strongest parts of a magnet are its **poles**. When a magnet is free to turn round, it lines itself up with the Earth's magnetic field. The pole that points north is called the north-seeking (or north) pole of the magnet. The pole that points south is called the south-seeking (or south) pole of the magnet.

4 Opposite magnetic poles attract each other (pull together) and similar poles repel each other (push away).

5 The direction of a magnetic field is always drawn in the direction of the force on the north-seeking pole of a magnet.

6 Every electric current has its own magnetic field.

7 An **electromagnet** is one that can be switched on and off. It is made by winding a coil of wire on an iron core.

8 The strength of an electromagnet can be increased by increasing the number of turns of wire or increasing the current in the coil.

9 An electric bell uses an electromagnet and a 'make and break' circuit to switch the electromagnet on and off repeatedly.

10 A **relay** is a switch that is operated by an electromagnet. It is used in applications where a small current or voltage is needed to switch on/off a large current or voltage.

---

**Key concepts**

- Similar magnetic poles repel each other; opposite magnetic poles attract each other.
- The arrows on a magnetic field pattern show the direction of the force on the north-seeking pole of a magnet.
- Magnets can attract and repel other magnets; they attract magnetic materials.

*The diagrams show the magnetic field patterns produced by a bar magnet and a current in a coil of wire.*

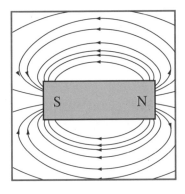
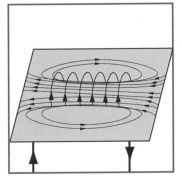

### Examiner's tip

When describing the action of a relay or electric bell, start by describing the effect of the current and then proceed in a logical order. For the relay shown in the diagram, the sequence is:

    the current in the coil is switched on;
    this creates a magnetic field;
    which magnetises the iron core;
    the iron armature is attracted to the iron core;
    causing the switch contacts to be pressed together.

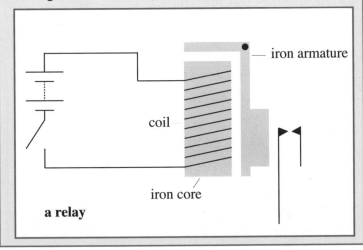

a relay

## Quick Questions

1. Which of the following materials are magnetic?
   **copper**
   **iron**
   **nylon**
   **polythene**
   **steel**

2. Does a magnet need to touch a magnetic material to attract it?

3. What name is given to the strongest parts of a magnet?

4. Complete the sentences:

   Two north-seeking poles _____ each other.

   Two south-seeking poles _____ each other.

   A north-seeking pole and a south-seeking pole _____ each other.

5. What do the arrows on a magnetic field pattern show?

6. What advantage does an electromagnet have over a fixed magnet?

7. Complete the sentence:

   An electromagnet is made by winding a coil of wire on an _____ core.

8. Write down two ways of increasing the strength of an electromagnet.

9. Which electromagnetic device uses a small current to switch a greater current?

10. Which electromagnetic device uses a 'make-and-break' circuit?

# What you need to know

**1** Two measurements are needed to calculate the speed of a moving object: the distance it travels and the time taken.

**2** The **speed** of a moving object is calculated using the formula:
speed = distance travelled ÷ time taken
When the distance is measured in metres (m) and the time is measured in seconds (s), the speed is in metres per second (m/s).

**3** An object stays at rest (not moving) or moves in a straight line at a constant speed if the forces on it are **balanced** (there are equal size forces acting in opposite directions).

**4** An **unbalanced force** is needed to start an object moving. The direction of motion is in the same direction as the unbalanced force.

**5** An unbalanced force acting on a moving object causes it to change speed or direction or both.

**6** For an object to increase its speed, the force in the direction of motion needs to be greater than the force in the opposite direction.

**7** For an object to slow down, the force that opposes motion must be greater than the force that causes motion.

**8** **Air resistance** and friction both act on moving objects.

**9** Air resistance always opposes motion through the air. The faster an object moves, the greater the air resistance force acting on it.

*The diagrams compare the driving and resistive forces on a moving cyclist. The cyclist on the left is speeding up, the one in the middle is travelling at a constant speed and the one on the right is slowing down.*

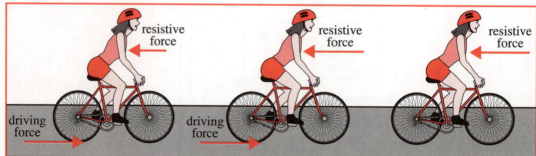

10 Friction opposes slipping and sliding. It is the force that stops shoes and wheels from slipping when walking or riding in a motor vehicle. It acts as a resistive force in bicycle and car brakes.

---

**Key concepts**

- Unbalanced forces cause a change in speed or the direction of motion.
- Speed is calculated using:
  speed = distance travelled ÷ time taken.
- The forces on an object are balanced when equal size forces act in opposite directions.

---

## Quick Questions

1 Which **two** measurements are needed to calculate the speed of a moving object?

2 Write down the formula used to calculate speed.

3 A driving force of 150 N acts on a cyclist. If the cyclist is moving at a constant speed and not changing direction, what is the size of the resistive force?

4 Name the force that stops cycle wheels from sliding on a road surface.

5 Name the resistive force that acts on a falling parachutist.

6 As a parachutist speeds up, how does the size of the resistive force change?

7 A sky diver opens her parachute and slows down. As she slows down, which force is greater, the Earth's pull or the air resistance?

8 When a car driver brakes, what is the direction of the resistive force on the car?

9 A bus sets off from a bus stop. What is the direction of the unbalanced force on the bus?

10 An archer fires an arrow. What force causes the arrow to start moving?

# What you need to know

**1** The effect that a force has in cutting or piercing is called **pressure**. The pressure caused by a force depends on both the size of the force and the area that it acts over.

**2** Drawing pins are designed to exert a large pressure by concentrating the force on a small area. This enables them to pierce.

**3** Skis are designed to exert a small pressure by spreading the force over a large area. This stops them from sinking in the snow.

**4** **Pressure** is calculated using the formula:
pressure = force ÷ area.
When the force is measured in newtons (N) and the area in square metres ($m^2$), the pressure is in newtons per square metre ($N/m^2$) or pascal (Pa).

**5** When an object turns, the centre of the rotation is called the **pivot**.

**6** The **moment** or turning effect of a force is a measure of how effective the force is at causing rotation.

**7** The turning effect of a force can be increased by increasing the size of the force or by moving its point of application further from the pivot.

**8** The moment or turning effect of a force is calculated using the formula:
moment = force × shortest distance to pivot.

**9** When the force is measured in newtons (N) and the distance in metres (m), the moment is measured in Nm.

*The diagrams show some effects of pressure and turning forces.*

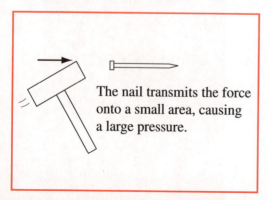

The nail transmits the force onto a small area, causing a large pressure.

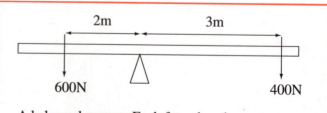

A balanced seesaw. Each force has the same moment but they are in opposite directions

**10** When an object, such as a balanced seesaw, is not turning, the sum of the clockwise moments equals the sum of the anticlockwise moments.
This is known as the **principle of moments**.

---

**Key concepts**

- Skis and caterpillar tracks on vehicles are designed to minimise the pressure by spreading the force over a large area
- Knives and scissors are designed to maximise the pressure by concentrating the force on a small area.
- The moment of a force is a measure of how effective it is in making things turn round.
  It is calculated using
  moment = force × shortest distance to pivot.
- Pressure describes the effect that a force has in cutting or piercing. It is calculated using
  pressure = force ÷ area.

---

**Examiner's tip**

Take care not to confuse the concepts of force and pressure. Force is a push or a pull. Pressure describes the effect that a force has when it acts on an object.

In response to the question 'Explain how a drawing pin is able to pierce a notice board', a common error is 'The pressure acts on a small area'. Here, the word 'pressure' has been used wrongly; it is the force that acts on a small area, causing a large pressure.

1 Why does a sharp knife cut better than a blunt one?

2 Why are heavy cranes fitted with caterpillar tracks instead of wheels?

3 What two measurements are needed to work out the pressure that a force causes?

4 Write down the two equivalent units of pressure.

5 Write down the formula for calculating pressure.

6 What is a pivot?

7 What two quantities does the turning effect of a force depend on?

8 State the principle of moments.

9 Write down the formula for calculating the moment of a force.

10 State the unit of the moment of a force.

# What you need to know

**1**   Light sources such as lamps, stars, television screens and flames give out light. They are seen when the light that they give out enters the eye.

**2**   Light normally travels at a constant speed in a straight line. It can change speed and direction when it passes from one material into another (see page 50).

**3**   Light travels much faster than sound. In air, the speed of light is one million times that of sound. This explains why some events can be seen before they can be heard.

**4**   Most objects reflect some of the light that falls on them.

**5**   Mirrors reflect light in a regular and predictable way. The angle between the incoming light and the mirror is equal to the angle between the reflected light and the mirror.

**6**   Other objects scatter some of the light that falls on them; the light is reflected in all directions.

**7**   Objects that are not light sources are seen when light scattered from them enters the eye.

**8**   **Shadows** are formed when light does not pass through an object but does pass by its edges and meets a screen.

**9**   A sharp shadow is formed by a point light source such as a torch lamp or the Sun (which appears to be a point source because it is a long way from the Earth).

**10** Fuzzy shadows are formed by extended light sources such as fluorescent tubes.

---

**Key concepts**

- Mirrors reflect light in a regular and predictable way.
- Light sources are seen by the light that they give out; other objects are seen by the light that they reflect.
- Light travels in a straight line, at a speed much faster than sound.

*The formation of sharp and fuzzy shadows*

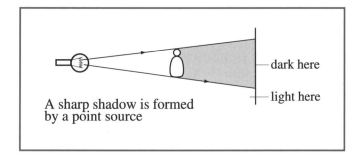

dark here

light here

A sharp shadow is formed by a point source

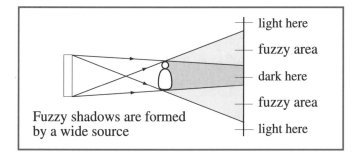

light here

fuzzy area

dark here

fuzzy area

light here

Fuzzy shadows are formed by a wide source

### Examiner's tip

When drawing the direction that light travels on a diagram, take care to make sure that the arrow points away from the light source and into the eye. A common error is to draw light coming out of the eye and being reflected back in. The diagram shows the correct way to draw light scattered from a book into the eye.

## Quick Questions

1  Which of the following give out light?
   **desk lamp**
   **kettle element**
   **mirror**
   **toaster**
   **sheet of paper**

2  Why can a low-flying aircraft be seen before it can be heard?

3  What is the rule connecting the angles when light is reflected at a mirror?

4  Complete the sentence. Normally, light travels in _____ lines.

5  Explain how you can read a book using the light from a bedside lamp.

6  Explain why you can see the picture on a television screen without any other light source.

7  What type of light source forms sharp shadows?

8  What type of light source forms fuzzy shadows?

9  Complete the sentence.
   When an object reflects light in all directions it _____ the light.

10  Name the two things that are needed for an object to form a shadow.

# What you need to know

1   When light crosses a boundary from one material into another there is a change in speed. This is known as **refraction**. Light slows down when passing from air into glass, water or plastic. It speeds up again as it passes back into air.

2   When the incident light is at right angles to the boundary between two materials there is no change in direction.

3   For other **angles of incidence**, light changes direction as it crosses the boundary. The direction of the light moves towards the normal line (a line drawn at right angles to the boundary) when the light slows down, and away from the normal line when it speeds up.

4   White light consists of a mixture of all the colours of the rainbow, from red to blue.

5   When light passes from air into glass, water or plastic, the different colours are split up; this is known as **dispersion**.

6   Dispersion can be seen when light travels through a triangular prism because the colours are separated both as the light enters and as it leaves the prism.

7   Red, green and blue are the **primary colours**; any other colour can be made by overlapping beams of these colours of light on a white screen, a process called **colour addition**. Televisions and computer monitors produce different colours by by mixing red, green and blue light in different proportions.

8   Cyan (turquoise), yellow and magenta (deep red) are the three **secondary colours**. Each is produced when beams of two primary coloured lights overlap on a white screen. Cyan is produced by overlapping blue and green, magenta by overlapping red and blue, and yellow when green light and red light overlap.

9   Colour **filters** can only remove colours from light. A filter of a primary colour allows its own colour through and absorbs light of the other two primary colours; this is called colour subtraction. A filter of a secondary colour allows through the two primary colours that make up its own colour and absorbs the third primary colour. The pigments in paints act in the same way.

10  When objects are viewed in different colours of light, they may appear to be different colours. They can only reflect light that is present in the light, so a red object cannot appear red when viewed in green or blue light.

## Key concepts

- When light is refracted, the change in speed may cause a change in direction of travel.
  The direction of travel moves towards the normal line when light slows down and away from the normal line when light speeds up.
- When light is dispersed by a prism it is split up into its constituent colours.
- Refraction describes the change in speed when light passes from one material to another.
- Coloured paints, colour filters and coloured objects remove colours from the light that reaches them. Each primary colour absorbs the other two primary colours and each secondary colour absorbs one of the primary colours.
- Mixing coloured lights on a screen is colour addition; mixing any two primary colours results in a secondary colour.

## Examiner's Tip

Working out the colour(s) that pass through a filter, or the colour that an object appears in coloured light is just like doing a simple subtraction sum. First, work out the primary colours present in the light. Then take away the primary colours absorbed by the filter or object. What is left is the colour(s) transmitted by the filter or reflected by the object.

*The diagrams show the dispersion as light passes through a triangular prism and the change in direction as light passes through glass.*

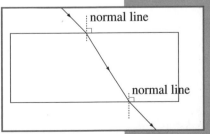

## Quick Questions

1 When light crosses a boundary between two materials there is a change in speed. What is the name of this effect?

2 Light passes from air into glass without changing direction. In what direction is the light travelling?

3 Light passes from air into glass and changes direction. Does the direction of travel move towards the normal line or away from the normal line?

4 White light can be split up into colours. What is the name of this effect?

5 Write down the three primary colours.

6 Write down the three secondary colours.

7 Describe how the colour yellow is produced on a television screen.

8 A green object is viewed in white light. Which of the primary colours does the object reflect?

9 Which two primary coloured lights could pass through a magenta filter?

10 An object looks blue when viewed in white light.
Explain why it looks black when viewed in red light.

# What you need to know

**1** Sound waves are caused by an object vibrating.

**2** Sound travels as vibrations of the particles in gases, solids and liquids. Sound is transmitted through windows and walls but it cannot travel in a vacuum.

**3** Sounds are heard when vibrations of the air cause the ear drum to vibrate. These vibrations are passed to the inner ear by three bones called the **ossicles**.

**4** The range of human hearing is from 20 Hz (20 vibrations per second) to 20 000 Hz, but not all people can detect sounds throughout this range.

**5** Exposure to loud sounds causes hearing loss by excessive wear of the ossicles. A very loud sound could cause permanent damage to the eardrum or the ossicles.

**6** The **amplitude** of a sound wave is the greatest distance that a vibrating particle moves from its rest position.

**7** The amplitude of a sound wave affects its loudness; the greater the amplitude, the louder the sound is heard.

**8** The **frequency** of a sound wave is the number of vibrations each second.

**9** The **pitch** of a sound is determined by its frequency. High-pitched sounds have a greater frequency than low-pitched ones.

---

**Examiner's tip**

Take care when drawing the traces that sound waves make on an oscilloscope screen. If the loudness is not changing, then the trace should maintain a constant height. If the frequency is not changing, then each complete vibration should occupy the same distance on the screen.

**10** An oscilloscope can be used to compare the amplitudes and frequencies of sound waves. It displays the number of waves that occur in a certain time interval.

*The diagrams show how changing the amplitude and frequency affect an oscilloscope trace of a sound wave.*

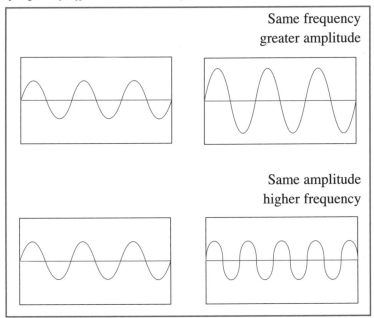

Same frequency
greater amplitude

Same amplitude
higher frequency

---

### Key concepts

- Increasing the amplitude of a sound wave makes it sound louder.
- Increasing the frequency of a sound wave makes it higher pitched.
- Sounds are caused by objects vibrating.
- They are transmitted by vibrations of the particles in solids, liquids and gases and are detected by vibrations of the ear drum.

## Quick Questions

1   How does a piano produce a sound?

2   Which of these can sound pass through?
**brick wall**
**glass window**
**empty space**
**wooden door**

3   Which part of the ear detects sound?

4   Name the bones that transmit vibrations to the inner ear.

5   Explain the meaning of the term amplitude.

6   Explain the meaning of the term frequency.

7   Which of the following frequencies are within the range of human hearing?
**10 Hz**
**100 Hz**
**1000 Hz**
**10 000 Hz**
**100 000 Hz**

8   How is hearing affected by exposure to loud sounds?

9   The volume of a radio is turned down. How does this affect the sound that it produces?

10  Two sounds have the same loudness but one is higher pitched. What is the difference between the two sound waves?

# What you need to know

1   The Sun is a star at the centre of the Solar System. It can be seen by the light that it gives out.

2   Planets orbit the Sun. They are kept in orbit by the attractive gravitational forces that exist between all masses. Planets can be seen by reflected sunlight.

3   Gravitational forces also keep moons and satellites in orbit around planets.

4   The further away a planet is from the Sun, the lower its orbital speed and the greater its orbital distance. This is why the length of a planet's 'year' depends on its distance from the Sun.

5   The four innermost planets are, in order of increasing distance from the Sun, Mercury, Venus, Earth and Mars.

6   The Sun rises in the eastern sky. It appears to move in an arc before it sets in the west. This apparent movement of the Sun is due to the Earth's daily rotation on its axis.

7   The Earth's daily rotation on its axis causes night and day. It also causes the stars to appear to rotate daily around the pole star. There is also an apparent annual rotation due to the Earth's movement around the Sun.

8   The Sun rises higher in the sky in summer than it does in winter. This is caused by the Earth being tilted on its axis; in our summer the northern hemisphere is tilted towards the Sun, making the days longer than in winter.

*The diagrams show the orbits of the three innermost planets and the gravitational forces between the Earth and the Moon.*

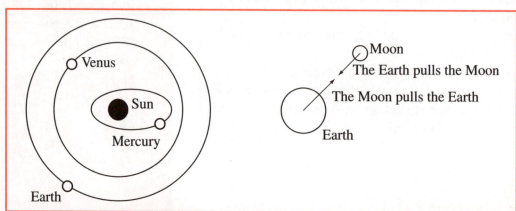

9   The orbit time of an artificial satellite depends on its distance from the Earth. Some weather satellites use low orbits that pass over the Earth's north and south poles. These make several orbits each day so that changes in weather can be monitored.

10  Some communications satellites (used for telephone, radio and television) have orbit times of 24 hours so that they stay over the same point on the Earth's surface. Artificial satellites are also used for navigation and surveillance.

---

### Examiner's tip

When explaining how planets, moons and satellites can be seen from the Earth, it is important to state clearly that light is reflected or scattered by the object. In response to the question 'Explain how the Moon can be seen from the Earth', an answer such as 'the Moon can be seen by the light that shines on it' would not gain a mark. An answer such as 'Light from the Sun is reflected by the Moon' would gain full marks.

---

### Key concepts

- The Earth rotates around the Sun once each year. This rotation is due to the attractive gravitational forces between the Earth and the Sun.
- The Sun is a star at the centre of the Solar System. It gives out light. Other objects in the Solar System are seen by the light from the Sun that they reflect.
- The Earth rotates on its axis once each day. At any time, half of the Earth is in darkness and half is lit up by light from the Sun.

## Quick Questions

1   Which object is at the centre of the Solar System?

2   Which planet is closest to the Sun?

3   Which two planets have a shorter year then the Earth's year?

4   Venus can sometimes be seen as a bright object in the sky. Explain how Venus can be seen from the Earth.

5   What type of force exists between the Sun and the planets?

6   What causes day and night?

7   Describe the difference in the Sun's position in the sky at noon on 20 December and at noon on 20 June.

8   Name two uses of artificial satellites.

9   How long does it take for the Earth to complete one orbit around the Sun?

10  Write down the names of two of the five outer planets.

# What you need to know

**1** We need an energy supply for food, transport and for heating, lighting and cleaning our homes. Everything that we do involves an **energy transfer**.

**2** Almost all our energy sources obtained their energy from the Sun. The exceptions are the energy in tides and in hot underground rocks (geothermal energy).

**3** Energy has been stored in the chemicals in **fossil fuels** such as coal, oil and gas for millions of years. They are **non-renewable** sources of energy as no more can be made in the lifetime of the Earth.

**4** Wood is a **renewable** fuel; when trees are cut down more can be grown. The wind and waves are driven by the Sun and tides are due mainly to the movement of the Moon around the Earth. They are also renewable sources of energy, as is the food that we eat.

**5** Most of the electricity generated in the UK comes from burning fossil fuels. Moving water in fast-flowing rivers and streams provides the energy for the generation of hydroelectricity in Scotland and Wales.

**6** Electricity cannot be stored directly. Surplus energy from electricity can be stored as gravitational potential energy when large quantities of water are raised from a low reservoir to a high reservoir. Releasing the water transfers this energy to **kinetic energy** as the water speeds up when falling down. The kinetic energy is transferred back to electricity as the fast-flowing water drives turbines.

**7** Energy can also be stored in the chemicals in batteries and transferred to electricity when needed. This is a particularly useful way for storing energy for use when the mains supply is not available.

**8** Domestic appliances transfer energy from electricity into heat, light and movement (including sound).

**9** Energy is always conserved, though some is usually wasted when a transfer of energy takes place. Most of the energy from electricity used for heating and doing other jobs in the home ends up as heat, raising the temperature of the surroundings by a small amount.

**10** Temperature measures how hot things are, not how much energy is stored in them. A bath full of water at 50°C stores a lot more energy than a spark from a sparkler at a temperature of 2000°C.

*The diagrams show some of the different ways in which objects can have energy. A moving train has kinetic energy; the cyclist gains gravitational potential energy as she travels up hill; the chemicals in the battery store energy; energy is also stored in chemicals in food.*

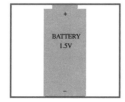 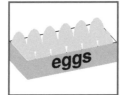

## Key concepts

- Most of the Earth's energy supply comes from the Sun.
- Everything that happens involves a transfer of energy. Although the total amount of energy stays the same, some of it is wasted and cannot be recovered.
- An energy source is renewable if it will not run out during the lifetime of the Earth.

## Examiner's tip

When an object travels vertically, there is usually transfer of energy between gravitational potential energy and kinetic energy. If a ball is thrown up in the air, energy is transferred from kinetic energy into gravitational potential energy. The opposite transfer occurs as the ball falls. A similar transfer takes place when a pendulum swings. In these cases the energy 'lost' is due to air resistance and ends up as heat in the air.

## Quick Questions

1 Which of these energy sources are renewable?
**coal**
**food**
**oil**
**wind**
**wood**

2 What is the source of the energy in the tides?

3 In one second, 60 J of energy from the electricity supply flows into a lamp. 4 J flows out as light. Explain what happens to the other 56 J of energy.

4 How is energy stored in batteries?

5 What type of energy is stored in the water in a reservoir near a hill top?

6 What type of energy does a moving object have?

7 Which requires more energy, heating a kettle full of water from 10°C to 100°C, or heating a bathful of water from 10°C to 50°C?

8 A hydroelectric power station generates electricity from the energy in moving water. What is the source of this energy?

9 Describe the energy transfer when an electric kettle is used to heat water.

10 Describe the energy transfer when a hairdrier is being used.

**1 (a)** A song thrush eats snails. The song thrush is called the predator and the snails are its prey. Eight different organisms are listed below:

**lion   spider   fish   earthworm   zebra   frog   heron   fly**

One predator-prey relationship from this list is spider – fly.
Write down two other predator-prey relationships. **[2]**

**(b)** The diagram shows a food web.

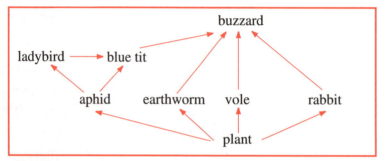

**(i)** Write down the food chain involving ladybirds. **[2]**

**(ii)** One hot summer the number of aphids increases rapidly.
Explain how this affects the number of ladybirds. **[2]**

**(iii)** A large number of rabbits are killed by disease.
Explain why this may have little effect on the number of buzzards. **[1]**

**(iv)** Explain why the death of a large number of rabbits may cause the ladybird population to increase. **[3]**

**2** The table gives the propoerties of four substances labelled W, X, Y and Z.

| property | W | X | Y | Z |
|---|---|---|---|---|
| Can you put your fingers through it? | ✗ | ✔ | ✔ | ✔ |
| Can it be poured? | ✗ | ✔ | ✔ | ✔ |
| Does it have a fixed shape? | ✔ | ✗ | ✗ | ✗ |
| Can it be squashed? | ✗ | ✗ | ✗ | ✔ |

Write out and complete these sentences using the table to help.

**(a)** W is a ................. because............................................................................. **[2]**

**(b)** Z is a ................. because............................................................................. **[2]**

**(c)** W and X are the same substance. Why can one be poured and the other cannot? **[2]**

**3** The diagram shows a narrow beam of white light reaching a prism.

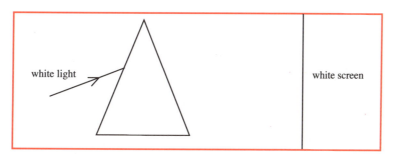

(a) Draw the path of the light through the prism to the screen. [2]

(b) Label the points on the screen where you would expect to see **red** light and **blue** light. [2]

(c) What is the name of the effect when white light is split into different colours? [1]

(d) A blue filter is placed in the path of the light before the prism.

    (i) Which of the three primary colours **red**, **green**, and **blue** can pass through the filter? [1]

    (ii) What is now seen on the screen? [1]

(c) Blue light is shone onto three different objects.
Complete the table below to show the colour that each object appears to be. [3]

| object | colour when viewed in white light | colour when viewed in blue light |
|---|---|---|
| ball | blue | |
| pen | red | |
| shoe | black | |

## Answers to quick questions

### Cells and organs

**1** Bladder. **2** The cell. **3** Nucleus and cytoplasm. **4** The cell membrane. **5** The chemical reactions of the cell. **6** To control which chemical reactions go on in the cell. **7** Two from: cellulose cell wall; chloroplasts and large central vacuole. **8** Because it is strong and supports the cell, helping it to keep its shape. **9** In chloroplasts. **10** It has a tail that enables it to move.

### Nutrition and circulation

**1** Proteins and vitamins. **2** It must meet the particular needs of that individual. **3** Because some foods do not contain all of the essential components. **4** Carbohydrates and fats. **5** Growth and repair. **6** Because the molecules are too big to be absorbed through cell membranes. **7** Because a very small quantity of enzyme will alter the rate of a chemical change and remain unchanged at the end of the reaction. **8** Through the large surface area of cells lining the small intestine. **9** Because we do not have the appropriate enzymes needed to digest those chemicals, e.g. we cannot digest cellulose because we do not have the enzyme cellulase. **10** They enable materials to get into and out of the blood stream.

## Movement

**1** Skull or vertebral column or rib cage. **2** Supports the body and provides anchorage points for muscles. Making red blood cells. **3** Tendons. **4** The bones are attached to each other by ligaments. **5** Knee. **6** A hinge joint can only enable movement in one plane whereas a ball and socket is more flexible, allowing movement in several planes. **7** Friction is increased making movement more difficult and painful. **8** Because a muscle can do work only when it contracts. Another muscle is needed to reverse the action of its partner in the antagonistic pair. **9** Biceps. **10** Scapula, humerus and ulna.

## Reproduction

**1** Testosterone. **2** Two from: breasts enlarge; hips widen; hair grows in armpits; pubic hair grows; eggs are released and periods start. **3** It provides nourishment and acts as a medium in which the sperm can swim. **4** Ovulation is the release of an egg from an ovary. **5** From the breakdown of the tissues lining the uterus. **6** To carry sperm from the testes to the penis. **7** Cervix → uterus → oviduct (Fallopian tube). **8** Oviduct (Fallopian tube). **9** It is the fusion of the nuclei of two different gametes, e.g. the nuclei of an egg and a sperm. **10** Nutrients present in the mother's blood pass across membranes in the placenta into the blood of the embryo.

## Breathing and respiration

**1** Mouth/nostril → nasal cavity → trachea → bronchi → bronchioles → alveoli. **2** Four from: large surface area; thin; moist; permeable to gases concerned; good blood supply close-by. **3** Pulmonary vein. **4** By diffusion. **5** They sweep mucus, containing small particles and bacteria, out of the air passages. **6** Tars. **7** To transport oxygen. **8** It is a compound formed when haemoglobin combines with carbon monoxide. **9** Glucose. **10** Glucose + Oxygen → Carbon dioxide + Water + Energy.

## Health

**1** Some compounds made by plants and animals function as drugs. Man-made compounds that copy the effects of these natural drugs, are called synthetic drugs. **2** Caffeine. **3** E.g. correcting fluid; hairspray; paintspray; solvent-based glues. **4** May induce violent behaviour. May lead to criminal activity as a means to finance the drinking. Drink-driving is a problem. **5** Microscopic organisms that cause disease. **6** Viral disease: e.g. influenza; bacterial disease: e.g. cholera. **7** To wash away any pathogens that might be present as a result of the wound occurring. Covering the wound reduces the chance of pathogens entering the wound later from the air or by other contact. **8** They try to destroy pathogens that have entered the body. **9** E.g. penicillin; actinomycin. **10** It either gives immediate protection against an infection or encourages the body's natural defence system to work. In the latter case, the body is then prepared should an infection occur later.

## Nutrition, growth and respiration

**1** Carbon dioxide and water. **2** Glucose. **3** Because it is used by plants and animals during aerobic respiration. **4** The Sun. **5** To trap light energy. **6** Palisade cells.

**7** Carbon dioxide + Water $\xrightarrow[\text{chlorophyll}]{\text{light}}$ Glucose + Oxygen **8** Nitrate ions.

**9** Because it is necessary for the synthesis of chlorophyll. **10** One wall of the cell is elongated to form a 'hair' that projects into and amongst the soil particles. The cell offers a large surface area for the absorption of water and mineral salts. The wall of the cell is thin.

## Reproduction

**1** To protect the inner parts of a flower when it is in bud.  **2** Male: stamen. Female: carpel.
**3** To produce male gametes (nuclei).  **4** They are large and colourful to attract pollinators (often insects).  **5** The transfer of pollen from a stamen to the stigma of a carpel.  **6** The stamens of wind-pollinated flowers have longer filaments than the stamens of insect-pollinated flowers. As a result their anthers hang outside the flower rather than remaining inside the flower as is the case in insect-pollinated flowers.  **7** Inside the ovule.  **8** It becomes a seed.  **9** The wall of the ovary changes after the ovules are fertilised. The modified ovary is then known as a fruit.  **10** Water; oxygen; an appropriate temperature ('warmth'); and in some cases, light.

## Variation, classification and inheritance

**1** Genetic and environmental.  **2** Genetic: eye colour. Genetic affected by environment: body mass.
**3** Body mass: genetics affected by environment. Eye colour: genetics. Number of fingers: genetics.
**4** Three from: prokaryotes; protoctists; fungi; plants; animals.  **5** Kingdom – phylum – class – order – family – genus – species.  **6** It is accepted practice to use a capital initial letter for the genus and a small initial letter for the specific name. The hippopotamus is therefore more correctly named: *Hippopotamus amphibius.*

**7**

| Group | Human |
|---|---|
| Kingdom | Animal |
| Phylum | Chordate |
| Class | Mammal |
| Order | Primate |
| Family | Hominid |
| Genus | *Homo* |
| Species | *sapiens* |

**8** When they breed animals and plants, humans may deliberately choose particular desirable characteristics or commercially beneficial features in the hope that these features will show up in the offspring. This is selective breeding.  **9** Resistance to fungal disease in wheat.  **10** Better egg-layers.

## Living things in their environment

**1** Because different habitats offer different combinations of environmental factors.  **2** Three from: temperature; amount of sunlight; rainfall (or snow or hail); wind strength.  **3** Three from: large size; fur; thick layer of body fat; ability to hibernate.  **4** Two from: deep or widespread root system; very small leaves or leaves reduced to spines; swollen stems; photosynthetic stems.  **5** Competition is the interaction between organisms for the resources found in their environment. E.g. Plants compete for space, light, water and mineral nutrients.  **6** E.g. Predator: owl. Prey: mouse.  **7** E.g. grass → sheep → man.  **8** Because they produce, from inorganic raw materials, the food on which they and all animals are dependant.  **9** Herbivores eat plants whereas carnivores eat other animals.  **10** The poisons may be eaten with the food, by herbivorous animals which in turn are eaten by carnivorous birds. The poison becomes more concentrated as it passes along the food chain and the carnivorous birds die.

## Solids, liquids and gases

**1** Liquid.  **2** Ice.  **3** 0°C.  **4** 100°C.  **5** More collisions between particles and walls.  **6** The particles move faster so more collisions.  **7** Sublimation.  **8** Diffusion.  **9** Particles are usually more closely packed in a solid than a liquid (exception: water).  **10** Ice.

### Elements, mixtures and compounds
**1** Elements.  **2** Oxygen.  **3** Use a magnet.  **4** Mixture of hydrogen and oxygen is a gas and water is a liquid.  **5** Copper and oxygen.  **6** Filtration.  **7** Chromatography.  **8** Fractional distillation.  **9** Hydrogen, sulphur and oxygen.  **10** $AlI_3$

### Metals and non-metals
**1** Mercury.  **2** Magnesium.  **3** Bromine.  **4** Hydrogen.  **5** Copper.  **6** An oxide.  **7** Non-metal.  **8** Metal.  **9** Metal.  **10** Malleable – beaten into a thin sheet. Ductile – drawn into a fine wire.

### Physical changes
**1** Ethanol.  **2** Tincture of iodine.  **3** Iodine.  **4** 110 g.  **5** Calcium carbonate reacts. If the resulting solution is evporated to dryness, calcium carbonate is not recovered.  **6** Less (because carbon dioxide gas has escaped).  **7** 130 g of solute would crystallise out (from each 100 g of solvent).  **8** Cold water expands when it turns to ice. This expansion can split the pipe.  **9** Sodium chloride.  **10** Potassium nitrate.

### Geological changes
**1** Granite.  **2** Marble.  **3** Chalk and limestone.  **4** Granite.  **5** Granite.  **6** The sharp-edged particles have rough edges knocked off by running water.  **7** The lower the rock, the older it is.  **8** The cooling of the liquid to form crystals was slow.  **9** Metamorphic.  **10** Glass and cement are two examples.

### Chemical reactions
**1** Mercury(II) oxide $\rightarrow$ mercury $+$ oxygen.  **2** (Thermal) decomposition.  **3** Lead(II) bromide $\rightarrow$ lead $+$ bromine.  **4** (Electrolytic) decomposition.  **5** Endothermic.  **6** Zinc oxide $+$ carbon $\rightarrow$ zinc $+$ carbon monoxide.  **7** Reduced.  **8** Oxidised.  **9** Reaction where oxidation and reduction take place.  **10** Natural gas power stations produce less pollution.

### Reactivity of metals
**1** Potassium.  **2** Silver.  **3** Between magnesium and zinc.  **4** Zinc + hydrochloric acid $\rightarrow$ zinc chloride $+$ hydrogen.  **5** No.  **6** Copper.  **7** Displacement.  **8** Copper(II) sulphate $+$ iron $\rightarrow$ copper $+$ iron(II) sulphate.  **9** Iron.  **10** Hydrogen.

### Acids and alkalis
**1** Hydrogen.  **2** Strong acid.  **3** pH 10.  **4** Sodium, hydrogen and oxygen.  **5** Carbon dioxide.  **6** pH7.  **7** To neutralise excess acidity.  **8** Atmosphere contains acid gases such as sulphur dioxide and oxides of nitrogen.  **9** To neutralise excess acid.  **10** Potassium nitrate.

### Electrostatics, current and charge
**1** friction  **2** electrons  **3** negative  **4** at the outside  **5** by losing electrons  **6** repulsive  **7** repulsive  **8** attractive  **9** electrons  **10** positive and negative ions

### Current in circuits
**1** Amp.  **2** Ammeter.  **3** Series.  **4** Parallel.  **5** Series.  **6** Equal to.  **7** None.  **8** 0.80 A  **9** Equal to 0.25 A.  **10** One.

### Magnetism
**1** Iron and steel.  **2** No.  **3** Poles.  **4** Repel; repel; attract.  **5** The direction of the force on the north-seeking pole of a magnet.  **6** It can be switched on and off.  **7** Iron.  **8** Increasing the number of turns of wire.  Increasing the current.  **9** Relay.  **10** Bell.

## Force and movement

**1** The distance travelled and the time taken. **2** Speed = distance travelled ÷ time taken. **3** 150 N. **4** Friction. **5** Air resistance. **6** It increases. **7** The air resistance. **8** Backwards (in the opposite direction to the motion). **9** Forwards. **10** The push of the string on the arrow.

## The effects of forces

**1** The force acts on a smaller area. **2** So that they exert a small pressure on the ground. **3** Force and area. **4** Pascal and newtons per square metre (Pa and $N/m^2$). **5** Pressure = force ÷ area. **6** The centre of rotation. **7** The size of the force and the shortest distance to the pivot. **8** When an object is not turning, the sum of the clockwise moments equals the sum of the anticlockwise moments. **9** Moment = force × shortest distance to pivot. **10** Nm.

## Seeing

**1** Desk lamp and toaster. **2** Light reflected from the aircraft travels much faster than the sound that it gives out. **3** The angle between the incoming light and the mirror is equal to the angle between the reflected light and the mirror. **4** Straight. **5** Light from the lamp is reflected by the book. Some of this light enters the eye. **6** The television screen gives out light. **7** A point source. **8** An extended source. **9** Scatters. **10** aalight source and a screen or surface to cast the shadow onto.

## Refraction and colour

**1** rrfraction. **2** At right angles to the surface (along the normal line). **3** Towards the normal line. **4** Dispersion. **5** Red, blue and green. **6** Cyan, yellow and magenta. **7** By a mixture of red light and green light. **8** Green. **9** Red and blue. **10** It does not reflect the red light.

## Sound

**1** The strings vibrate. **2** Brick wall, glass window and wooden door. **3** The ear drum. **4** The ossicles. **5** The greatest distance moved from the rest position. **6** The number of vibrations per second. **7** 100 Hz, 1000 Hz and 10 000 Hz **8** It causes loss of hearing. **9** The amplitude is reduced. **10** The higher pitched sound has a higher frequency.

## The Earth and beyond

**1** The Sun. **2** Mercury. **3** Mercury and Venus. **4** Light from the Sun is reflected by Venus. **5** Gravitational. **6** The Earth's rotation on its axis. **7** The Sun is higher in the sky in June than it is in December. **8** Any two from: monitoring the weather; communications; looking into space; navigation; surveillance. **9** 365 days. **10** Two from: Jupiter; Saturn; Neptune; Uranus; Pluto.

## Energy

**1** Food, wind and wood. **2** The Moon and the Sun. **3** It flows out as heat. **4** In the chemicals as chemical energy. **5** Gravitational potential energy. **6** Kinetic energy. **7** Heating the bathful of water. **8** The Sun. **9** Energy is transferred from electricity into heat. **10** Energy is transferred from electricity to heat and movement.

# Answers to sample questions

**1 (a)** Any two from: lion and zebra; heron and frog; heron and fish; heron and worm; frog and fly; frog and worm; frog and spider; fish and worm. **(b) (i)** Plant → aphid → ladybird. **(ii)** Ladybirds eat aphids, therefore ladybird population should increase. **(iii)** Because buzzards can eat other organisms, e.g. voles. **(iv) Either** buzzards eat rabbits, therefore buzzards eat blue tits instead, therefore fewer ladybirds predated, **or** fewer plants eaten, therefore more food available supporting more aphids, therefore more ladybirds survive.

**2 (a)** Solid, because it has a fixed shape but cannot be squashed or poured and you cannot put your fingers through it. **(b)** Gas, because it has not got a fixed volume and can be squashed. **(c)** X is a powder. The tiny pieces of solid are not joined and will pour like a liquid.

**3 (a)** See diagram to right.

   **(b)** See diagram to right. **(c)** Dispersion.

   **(d) (i)** Blue. **(ii)** Blue light only.

   **(e)** Blue, black, black.

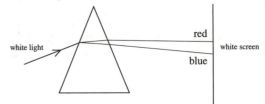

Letts Educational
Aldine Place
London W12 8AW
Tel: 020-8740 2266
Fax: 020-8743 8451
e-mail: mail@lettsed.co.uk
website: http://www.lettsed.co.uk

First published 1999
Reprinted 1999 (twice)
Text, design and illustrations: © BPP (Letts Educational) Ltd 1999

Prepared by *specialist* publishing services, Milton Keynes

**British Library Cataloguing in Publication Data**
A CIP record for this title is available from the British Library.

Printed in Italy

ISBN 1 85758 914 9

Letts Educational is the trading name of BPP (Letts Educational) Ltd